CULT
HEROES

MANCHESTER CITY

CULT HEROES

MANCHESTER CITY

David Clayton

This edition first published by Pitch Publishing 2012

Pitch Publishing
A2 Yeoman Gate
Yeoman Way
Durrington
BN13 3QZ
www.pitchpublishing.co.uk

A CIP catalogue record is available for this book
from the British Library

PB: ISBN 978-1-9080516-4-6
HB: ISBN 978-1-9080519-9-8

Typesetting and origination by Pitch Publishing.

Printed in Great Britain by TJ International.

Contents

Acknowledgements

This, I believe is the hardest project I've ever undertaken and the research involved has taken up endless evenings and nights. To that end, I'd like to thank my wife Sarah and my children Harry, Jaimé and Chrissie for allowing me to get on with my work and limiting my precious time with them.

Thanks to all the City fans that aired their opinions on who they believed was a Cult Hero and who wasn't – I soaked up all the various arguments for and against in shortlisting the final 20.

I'd also like to thank all the unaccredited reporters whose clippings I sifted through over the past years. Many were so old they crumbled on touch – the clippings, not the reporters – and Eric Todd and Eric Thornton, in particular, recorded moments, recounted in the following pages which might have otherwise been forgotten forever.

I would like to thank the publisher, of the original hardback edition, Simon Lowe, for his patience and encouragement and Paul Camillin for republishing it in paperback.

Lastly, thanks to Shaun Wright-Phillips for writing the foreword. Much appreciated!

David Clayton

For Chrissie, my baby daughter.

Daddy's home

xxx

Foreword

by Shaun Wright-Phillips

When David Clayton approached me to write the foreword to 'Manchester City's Cult Heroes' I was happy for a number of reasons.

The fact that I am one of the 20 players he'd selected is one of them and if other City fans feel the same way, I'll feel even happier. Another reason is that this introduction is a chance for me to say thanks to the City fans for all the support they gave me during my time at Maine Road and the City of Manchester Stadium. I enjoyed every day I played for the club and if the fans remember me fondly I can assure you it is reciprocated.

If I am a kind of Cult Hero, it's down to hard work, belief and the backing I had from the supporters, who were with me from day one and right up to the day I joined Chelsea – that's something I won't ever forget. I think to be a hero at City, you need to play with your heart each time you go out and if the paying customers see you giving your all, they'll back you all the way.

Looking at some of the other players in the book, a lot of them were before my time, but I have at least heard of most of them. I was lucky enough to play alongside the likes of Shaun Goater, Andy Morrison and Ali Benarbia, who are all included in this book and it's not hard to understand why their popularity will continue for years to come.

As for me, I'd be hard pressed to pick out just one happy memory from my time with City because there are so many. My first goal at Millwall was special, and I loved scoring my goals against Manchester United, particularly the one I struck in the 4-1 at the City of Manchester Stadium, which I think I'm safe in saying, went down well with the supporters, too...

I learned my trade at City and I'll be forever grateful for the belief and encouragement the club showed in me during my time there. I became an England player with City and I'll always have a special place for the club and the supporters in my heart.

If I'm still thought of as a Cult Hero in another 10 years, you won't find me complaining.

Shaun Wright-Phillips

Introduction

How can you possibly decipher who is a Cult Hero and who is a Club Legend and have everyone agree with the 20 selections permitted? The answer is simple, you can't. What can be put forward, however, is an argument to what makes one player a terrace idol and another some kind of untouchable deity.

In truth, the latter are few and far between and the only three I believe quality without question, I have therefore omitted, namely Mike Summerbee, Colin Bell and Francis Lee – the Holy Trinity. I thought long and hard about their inclusion in this book but ultimately decided against it. Their legendary status is without question and they will be immortal heroes as long as Manchester City FC exists.

Would their inclusion have added a few extra sales? Maybe, but Buzzer, The King and Franny have already had reams of pages written about them elsewhere and I wasn't sure what I could add that would be of interest or would be original. I'm not prepared to regurgitate old material, and besides, I had to draw the line of what qualified as a Cult Hero and what didn't.

It's my opinion that there has to be some element of controversy involved in their time at the club and if they began with the crowd not initially taking to them, so much the better. That they won a legion of admirers by the time their days in sky blue and white had finished is justification enough.

I think Bert Trautmann, Shaun Goater, Rodney Marsh, Billy Meredith, Joe Corrigan, Mike Doyle, Uwe Rosler, Andy Morrison, Clive Allen, Andy Morrison and even Roy Paul all fit into that category, or have done at least at some point in their career.

Gerry Gow is included because he hit them hard and we loved it and for all the Blues' reputation for having purveyors of the Beautiful Game among their ranks, the truth is, they are few and far between and the sight of a bone-crunching tackler fighting the cause evokes just as much emotion as a mazy dribble or defence-splitting pass. Think about some of the club's most popular players of the past 30 years, for instance, and it's safe to say a fair proportion of them will be tough-tackling leaders on the pitch.

Frank Swift, Dennis Tueart could effortlessly slip into the Club Legend section –so why didn't they? Swifty's era clinched his place and the stories about how he was with the supporters and what he meant to them at the time make up my favourite chapter in this book. Tueart's place in the club's history is assured, but I sometimes feel he isn't quite given the credit he deserves. He was a major player for the Blues in the 1970s and a huge favourite of the excited kids who watched him from the white Kippax perimeter walls – yours truly included.

Ian Bishop, Trevor Francis, Georgi Kinkladze and Ali Benarbia were all Tuesday's children – full of grace – and were conductors of an orchestra that often played out of tune. When the music was good, though, it was the sweetest, most angelic sound you could ever hear. I think their inclusion was mandatory and while I don't think too many would consider them as legends, few would argue they weren't Cult Heroes.

Paul Lake and Shaun Wright-Phillips make up the 20 – Lake tagged as the next Colin Bell and with a career-ending injury that matched the great man, is not only revered for the games he did play, but the thought of those he should have played and where that might taken him and City.

Wrighty was a breath of fresh air who made Saturday afternoons exciting, expectant occasions. He overcame his own hurdles to become adored by the City faithful for his attitude and endeavour.

But what of those who aren't included? Arguments could be presented for the entire 1968 championship side, but would that make fascinating, varied reading? That's for the reader to decide. Tony Coleman came the closest to being included from

Joe Mercer's all-conquering team, but Doyle and Corrigan were ultimately the only representatives, and then mainly because they spanned two successful eras. From the stars of the seventies, Asa Hartford, Peter Barnes and the magnificent Dave Watson weren't far off either, and Brian Kidd, Joe Royle and Gary Owen had strong cases.

In later years, David White, Niall Quinn, Peter Beagrie, David Rocastle, Marc Vivien Foe and Paul Walsh went under the microscope and may well be certainties to fill other City fans' lists.

Tony Coton, Neil McNab, Clive Wilson, and Alex Williams all served the club with great distinction and again, all merited inclusion. Sometimes it was a straight fight with another player of their era – Goater v Paul Dickov, for instance, Benarbia v Eyal Berkovic... the list goes on – trust me. In truth, it's virtually impossible to select just 20 players from 125 years of football at City and the more than 1,000 players who've worn the jersey with varying degrees of success.

Johnny Crossan, Dave Wagstaffe, Kaziu Deyna, Dave Ewing, Sam Cowan, Eric Brook, Tom Johnson, Derek Kevan. Even Maurizio Gaudino and Trevor Morley almost made the final cut. The problem really wasn't who to include, but who to leave out.

In the following chapters, I've hopefully put up a decent argument as to why the 20 players I've chosen are there, but no doubt everyone will have their own opinions. What is important is that you enjoy the book and reliving certain moments that these players have been involved in and, in some cases, learning something new about them in the process. If you have half as much fun reading Cult Heroes as I've had writing it, I'll be satisfied with that, even if you don't agree with them all.

David Clayton

Billy Meredith

1894-1906 & 1921-1924: 393 games, 151 goals

THE FOOTBALL CLUB that would eventually become Manchester City stumbled into life in early 1880 as St. Mark's of West Gorton, thanks to two wardens of St. Mark's church in that district of East Manchester. The fledgling club played their home games on what was described as 'a piece of rough ground' on Clowes Street. Their first game ended in a 2-1 defeat to Baptist Church of Macclesfield – both teams fielded 12 men.

A year later they were renamed West Gorton (St. Mark's) and three years after that they became plain old Gorton. Next on the new names list, following a move to a new ground just to the east of Manchester city centre, was Ardwick FC (the name the club entered the Football League under, being deemed worthy enough to be one of the founder members of the Second Division) and, after something of a financial crisis, they finally re-formed as the far catchier Manchester City in 1894.

How fitting then, that the club's first Cult Hero should also join City that year.

Billy Meredith's tale is completely fascinating and that he became a superstar of his day was no surprise to any of his legion of admirers, but his somewhat chequered stay with the Blues would become the stuff of legend for mostly the right reasons, but several wrong ones, too. Indeed, the man from North Wales very nearly destroyed the club who'd given him the platform to become a hero to thousands. In short, Meredith and City were made for each other and when they were together, it was a heady cocktail of sublime talent and skulduggery.

BORN IN THE North Wales border village of Chirk on 30 July 1874, Billy Meredith was just five-years-old when St. Mark's of West Gorton were formed. He was taught and encouraged to play football by a local headmaster, T. E. Thomas, who presided over a school that produced no less than 49 internationals. The secret behind that phenomenal success? Thomas was also treasurer of the Welsh FA and obviously knew raw talent when he saw it.

It may well be the case that Thomas honed Meredith's skills, along with those other internationals, with his most famous training technique. The teacher used to stress the value of ball practice to his charges and would place a penny in the far end of the schoolyard with the boy who kicked the ball nearest to the coin being allowed to keep it as a prize. Thomas, clearly a man before his time in an era when kick and rush was the order of the day as the game had barely evolved from its frantic roots, also stressed the importance of keeping the ball on the ground. During practice in the schoolyard, anyone who kicked the ball over the wall would be sent straight back to lessons as punishment – no wonder his methods were embraced wholeheartedly by a succession of youngsters.

Meredith's natural talent saw him debut for local side Chirk's reserve team aged 16, whilst working as a pit pony driver at Black Park colliery. By 18 he starred for the first team as they reached the Welsh Cup final, only losing 2-1 to Wrexham. A year later Chirk lifted the trophy for the fifth time in their history. At the start of the next season, 1894/95, Meredith scored 11 goals in three games. He had outgrown the Welsh League.

Meredith's wanderlust saw him yearning to perform on a bigger stage and he travelled to Cheshire to play for Northwich Victoria, who, having lost their place in the Second Division in 1894, the year that City were renamed, entered the Welsh Cup and had a reputation for scouting local talent. One early opinion on Meredith from Northwich officials was that he was not only pale and puny, but "too bloody slow." They saw no purpose in his sleight of foot and outwitting of opponents when kick and rush was the order of the day. Such is the burden of blossoming genius.

They also believed him to be a show-off, hugging the touchline close to the spectators with a trademark toothpick in his mouth – the latter was a replacement for a chewing tobacco habit he'd acquired whilst down the pits. These views, typical of an era where stuff and nonsense were definitely not the order of the day, were, however, quickly disregarded by more knowledgeable souls at the club and Meredith soon became a favourite with the faithful during his short stay – just half-a-dozen matches – at Drill Field.

But there was much more to Meredith than a few flashy displays for the Vics – he was a miner who put in solid 70-hour weeks, then would either cycle or make the 60-mile journey to Cheshire by bus – yes, that previous sentence did include the word 'cycle' – to play football... for free. When old timers insist that footballers back in days gone by were 'real men', chances are they had Billy Meredith or one of his equals in mind.

WITH NO NETWORK of scouts watching promising talent around the country in the late 19th century, it was an incredible stroke of luck that in October 1894, one Lawrence Furniss happened to be refereeing a game at Northwich in which Billy Meredith was playing. Furniss had heard of Meredith's repute from two former Chirk players who now wore the blue of Ardwick and he couldn't help but be impressed by the tall, willowy figure on the wing who left a trail of players tacking fresh air before either presenting a chance to a team-mate or slotting home the ball himself. If you're wondering how an impressed referee could possibly advantage Second Division Manchester City, perhaps the fact that he was destined to become the club chairman might answer the question. Furniss talked to club officials about the young winger and he and two club representatives were soon on the train travelling to the tiny Denbighshire village of Chirk on a mission to secure the services of this talented 19-year-old.

They sought out Meredith, well known among locals in the tiny, close-knit community and found their surprised quarry a little non-plussed at all the fuss he was causing. Typically for such a clean-cut Victorian hero, Billy declared he didn't want to turn professional because he wasn't comfortable taking money for doing what he loved best, but he agreed to become a Manchester City player all the same, and if the three club officials had smiles the sizes of Cheshire cats on the return journey to Manchester, who could have blamed them? They'd just secured the services of possibly the greatest player in the world at that moment in time – with the development of the global game at that stage embryonic at best, saying that Meredith was one of the world's best is no overstatement.

CITY HAD A decent ground by this time at Hyde Road, but what the loyal, if not yet vast, band of supporters didn't realise was that Meredith was going to spearhead the club's driving ambition to become one of the biggest and best in England; at least, not yet anyway.

Football at this time was a mix of enthusiastic amateurs and the first hard-working professionals, with the former greatly outnumbering the latter. Gate receipts, such as they were, would barely cover the running costs of clubs up and down the country and on one occasion a City spectator paid a gatekeeper half-a-crown for admittance (several times greater than the admission fee) and told him to keep the change for the benefit of the club. The man was sought, thanked and invited on to the board – and no, he wasn't Roman Abramovic's great grandfather. According to club records, the mysterious benefactor declined the offer, but was flattered, nonetheless.

The late 1880s and early 1890s had seen the formation of several soon-to-become Lancashire giants and City's first fixture list (as MCFC) would include the likes of Newcastle United, Woolwich Arsenal, Bury and Notts County. Bolton Wanderers, Blackburn Rovers and Preston North End resided in the division above. City had been in existence officially for just six months when Meredith signed and the crowds were growing as football gripped the city. Prior to that, the unthinkable – rugby – had been Manchester's favourite sport, but in a place described as having 'poor visibility in daylight', it was perhaps only right that a sport that, by and large, played the ball along the ground and didn't necessarily come down covered in soot, should enrapture the working class of the day.

Though exact figures gave way to estimates when it came to counting the attendance, City's generally varied between 2,000 and 5,000. Meredith made his debut on 27 October 1894 at to Newcastle United's St James' Park in front of approximately 2,000 people during a fabulous 5-4 see-saw game. His home debut a week later was played in front of City's biggest gate to date – 14,000 – and resulted in a 5-2 win for Newton Heath, soon to become Manchester United. The derbies had begun in earnest and Meredith had just won himself about 10,000 new admirers by scoring both City's goals.

Interest was growing at a phenomenal rate and, in Meredith, those new to football instantly identified a hero who was also one of their own – a working class lad who earned his crust during the week, then turned out and gave his all for his club – taking nothing for the privilege. He scored 12 goals in 18 games in that first season, becoming a full-time pro towards its end when the constant entreaties of City's board finally won the day and he ended his association with his hometown pit. Released from the burden of labour and able to train full-time, Billy's second season, 1895/96, saw him miss just one game, score another dozen from the wing and almost inspire the team to promotion, but back then the runners-up spot in Division Two was not good enough.

The gates against rivals Newton Heath got bigger – 20,000 packing in to Hyde Road – and Meredith was now popular around the country, with the Welshman famed for rarely being seen without a beloved toothpick jutting from the corner of his mouth.

He wasn't bad at football either. In 1898, Meredith began the campaign with a hat-trick – one of four that season – and his incredible 29 goals in 33 games helped the Blues to their first major honour, the Second Division championship in April 1899. This was the first season of automatic promotion between the two divisions. Previously various mixtures of straight promotion, election and test matches had resolved such issues, but City went up as the first ever automatically promoted champions of Division Two – and they were led there by the dazzling skills of Billy Meredith.

He would hug the touchline and draw his victims in before dropping a shoulder and leaving them tackling a recent memory. Journalists, like the general public, were enraptured by his ability to back-heel a cutting through-ball or whip in swerving shots from all angles – and this with an often sodden leather ball that is perhaps twice the weight of today's equivalent. He was labelled as the 'Prince of Wingers' in newspaper reports and he missed only seven games in his first five years at City, three because of playing for Wales and one because his train from Chirk was stopped by fog – god knows what prevented him playing in the other three games but chances are it would leave most mortals on death's door!

Moving up a level didn't diminish Billy's effectiveness and he managed another 14 goals during the club's first season in the top flight. Twice matches were played in front of 25,000-plus as football continued to prosper, but City then began to struggle and by 1902 they had been relegated. The infamous yo-yo existence of the club which was to plague its fans from that day to this, had begun.

Setting another trend which lasts until today, supporters became restless and demanded a meeting with the board of directors where frank views were expressed and demands made, but there was a depression surrounding the club that was proving difficult to shake off. Meredith, a bright and intelligent chap, noted to friends that there were few smiles after matches and his team-mates seemed afraid to laugh or crack jokes and that he would change as quickly as possible after a game and head home rather than be in such a sapping atmosphere. Today, of course, Meredith could have simply slapped in a transfer request and sat on some flash London club's bench for the next couple of seasons, but that wasn't the way things were done back then – in fact the real dramas of Billy's stay at City lay just around the corner.

During the summer of 1902 the under-fire board spent £1,497 on reinforcements and, with the influx of new talent, City won promotion at the first attempt. Sandy Turnbull, who arrived from his Scots hometown club of Hurlford Thistle, and Billy Gillespie weighed in with plenty of goals to bolster Meredith's wizardry and the trio bagged 64 goals in 88 games between them. The omens were good and the black cloud that had hung heavy over Hyde Road for the past few years dissipated to be replaced by unbridled optimism – and with good reason. 1903/04 was to be the best in the young club's history and almost resulted in an historic double. Meredith was an ever-present as City chased their first top-flight title and, though they narrowly finished runners-up to Sheffield Wednesday, the Blues had their revenge in the FA Cup semi-final at Goodison Park as they beat Wednesday 3-1 to progress to their first Cup final. The historic game, against local rivals Bolton Wanderers, was played at The Crystal Palace, London, in front of 61,374 fans and the only goal of the game was scored by, well, even an educated guess is surely not required to assume that crowd favourite Billy Meredith bundled home a controversial winner. The opposition were convinced Meredith was well offside when he was put through for a one-on-one – but that's opposition for you, especially when it's cost their side the Cup final. Meredith had, by this time, become City captain, given the honour at the callow age of 21, and to be presented with the FA Cup by Lord Alfred Lyttelton having just been voted the most popular player in the country by readers of *The Umpire*, was a truly memorable occasion.

The classicly moustached Meredith was at the zenith of an incredible popularity. He not only commanded the hearts of City fans on the field, but he drew huge crowds to any public event he attended up and down the country.

There were several late-Victorian sporting superheroes. W.G. Grace, the famously bearded cricketer, cross-discipline genius C.B. Fry, who played football, cricket, rugby, and even held the world long jump title, and the incredible Captain Matthew Webb, the first man to swim the English Channel and purveyor of incredible swimming feats at baths across the country, who would eventually meet his end trying to swim over Niagara Falls. But Billy Meredith was one of only two footballers who could truly claim a place amidst such a pantheon of greats. He and Sheffield United goalkeeper William 'Fatty' Foulke, were the only two to become anything like household names in a sport which still had not become the all-consuming passion of the masses, or of the country's newspaper scribes. Football was well on the way, though as City and Billy's reception back home proved.

Manchester went crazy. The triumphant tour of town was attended by tens of thousands, with the biggest cheers reserved for the returning hero Meredith. The pubs were packed as City fans let down their hair and celebrated long into the night and the club, growing at a rate of knots hardly thought possible, had proved they were arguably the best in the country. Loved by youngsters and adults alike, wherever Meredith played the crowds flocked to see him and with his distinctive toothpick and bandy legs, the outside-right who could deliver pinpoint crosses, possessed a thunderous shot and an exquisite back-heel, was a cartoonist's delight.

BUT DISASTER, IN football terms, was about to strike. It always seems to have been the way at Manchester City. The pattern has been repeated consistently for over 100 years. On this occasion the club were effectively about to take a sawn-off shotgun and point both barrels at its foot. For Billy Meredith, it was to be a time of naivety and notoriety that only his incredible popularity would eventually rescue him from.

In October 1904, five City directors were found guilty of paying players illegal payments and it was revealed there were also irregularities involving transfer deals with Glossop North End. The five were duly suspended for three years, while the team was banned from playing at home for a month. As if that wasn't bad enough, the following year, as City chased a first-ever league title, the FA suspended Meredith for three years for attempting to bribe Aston Villa's captain – A. Leake, apparently, though, with a name like that, it was probably reasonable to believe the man couldn't keep secrets. The £10 inducement offered before a vital match during the championship run-in was apparently to ensure City win the game. It seems fairly paltry given that it would have had to be spread between the other members of the team for it to have had the desired effect. Meredith claimed to have acted on behalf of an unnamed club official, but the ban was imposed upon him all the same. Things got worse when he demanded the club continue to pay his wages while under the suspension from playing and then visited the dressing rooms on a matchday – he was now prohibited from entering. City had had their fill of the Welsh Wizard and placed Meredith on the transfer list.

Cast into the wilderness and a personal hell sure to lead to damnation, where more appropriate for pariah Meredith to find himself but Manchester United, who snapped him up for just £500, well aware he wouldn't be available for a further two years, but safe in the knowledge they'd just secured a deal that was almost a cast-iron guarantee of landing silverware, as well as relieving their deadly rivals of their best player.

The repercussions were serious for City too. With 17 other players banned until 1907 and barred from ever playing for the club again, the Blues effectively lost their playing staff and, due to an investigation which uncovered that City's top stars such as Meredith had been illegally earning £6 per week, more than twice the amount earned by factory or mine workers, but £2 above the maximum limit imposed by the FA for professionals, most of the officials too.

City somehow avoided relegation, despite losing the first two matches of 1905/06 4-1 and 9-1, but Manchester United laughed all the way to the bank by signing on the pick of City's banned heroes, including Sandy Turnbull, who would go on to score over 100 goals for the club, Herbert Burgess and Jimmy Bannister. From having a team that could take on and beat anyone with the best and most inspirational player in the country as its captain, City had been reduced to fielding a team of reserves and youngsters. The FA, determined to make an example and set a precedent for a deterrent in their punishments, had severely punished the club. It is almost certainly during this period that the phrase 'typical City' was first uttered and it's definitely where the origins of unpredictability and self-destruction which beset every City fan on the planet in the early 21st century originate.

As for the beleagured supporters, they didn't know which way to turn. While the hatred of all things emanating from Old Trafford certainly wasn't quite as vitrolic as it is today, there was still dismay and anger from the people who really did pay the players' wages back then, but finding a scapegoat would prove nigh on impossible, with so many culprits to point the finger at. Meredith was still a legend and the fans had difficulty in turning him into the villain of the piece. People generally accepted their lot, back then, and after the intial disappiontment, the masses got back to doing what they did best - supporting their club. Some suggested the north-south divide had been highlighted with the severity of the Blues' punishment handed out by the London-based FA, but as there were few other cases to compare, life went on.

PERHAPS NOT SURPRISINGLY Meredith was unhappy at his treatment by football's governing body, but, being a forthright and determined character, he remained an influence on the game – even if he couldn't actually play. It was Billy's persistence that saw the formation of the first Players' Union, the forerunner of the Professional Footballers' Association. Upon its formation in 1907, Billy was quoted as saying: "What is more reasonable than that our plea that the footballer, with his uncertain career, should have the best money he can earn? If I can earn £7 a week, should I be debarred from receiving it?" He truly was a man well before his time in so many ways.

Meredith even used his influence to change the rules regarding penalty kicks. Up to that point, a keeper could stand several yards off his line when a spot-kick was about to be taken. Meredith felt this law was ridiculous, and had set about proving it so by simply scooping the ball over a keeper's head when taking a penalty. The FA agreed and from 1906 the custodian was forced to stay on his line for penalty kicks.

Meredith and the authorities crossed swords again in 1909 when the FA required players to sign contracts which disowned Meredith's brainchild, the Players' Union. A major battle for the hearts and minds of professionals emerged, with the union demanding an end to the restrictive maximum wage. The affair led to threats of strikes, lockouts, postponed matches and underhand tactics adopted by both sides in their determination to win. The Manchester United players, marshalled by Billy, were most conspicuous in their demands and fortitude. Eventually, the dispute was settled when the FA dropped their demand, and the union, after a ballot of members, chose not to become a member of the General Federation of Trade Unions, the forerunner of the modern Trades Union Congress.

TO MAKE MATTERS worse for City, after his ban was lifted on 31 December 1906, Meredith enjoyed a successful 15-year stay with Manchester United, who he helped win two league championships (1907/08 & 1910/11) and the FA Cup (1909), plus lift the first ever Charity Shield in 1908 and win it again in 1911. In 1912 Meredith was awarded a testimonial game and he chose to play a game against Manchester City. Despite the tainted history, in April over 39,000 fans turned up to pay tribute to the City's greatest ever footballer. The game brought in receipts of £1,400. It was an incredible show of support for Billy and proved his enduring appeal to City fans and further proved that they apportioned little or no blame for the dramatic events of the past few years.

His success at Old Trafford, where United moved from their old Bank Street ground in February 1910, afforded him not only further nationwide status as a top sportsman, but also as one who could transcend the kind of deep divides which exist between supporters of two fierce rival clubs. Imagine Franny Lee trying to leap that chasm in the early 1970s, or Bryan Robson in the 1980s and Keane, Cantona or Goater in the modern era. Ridiculous. Picture Keegan wearing the blue of Everton or Patrick Vieira sporting the cockerel of Spurs. One only has to ask the likes of George Graham, Sol Campbell, Mo Johnston, Harry Redknapp and David Mellor what it's like to run the gauntlet of hate thrown down by both sets if supporters when crossing deeply-entrenched positions in very local disputes. Yet that's what Meredith was able to achieve.

GRANTED, THE LINES were not so starkly drawn and there was not yet such history between the two Manchester clubs and their respective supporters, but nonetheless Billy circumvented all of that ill-feeling which did exist either from those who did not want to lose him on the blue side of the city, to those who may not want a shamed City reject on the red.

In later years others tried to bridge the divide; Denis Law famously failed to celebrate like a true blue would when condemning United to the drop in 1974 and Peter Barnes was another to play for both clubs. In more recent years, Terry Cooke, Jon Macken, Andy Cole and even Shaun Goater represented both Manchester giants at some level with varying degrees of success but it has been an age since the Blues bought a player directly from the Reds and one who was considered an important first-team regular and vice-versa – both boards know it is simply unacceptable.

Billy Meredith did have his own uncrossable divide to bear. He openly admitted that he was unfortunate that his international career could not match that of his club achievements and once said: "I wish that I had been born in England. You know the house I was born in was only 300 yards or so over the border. What a time I should have I had if had been an Englishman. I'm sick of being on the losing side." Sentiments echoed by millions of Englishmen who would have loved to have seen Meredith in a white shirt!

It was at the end of hostilities that Meredith was to put an end to the hoodoo. Wales entertained England in what was called a 'Victory International' at Cardiff on 11th October 1918. Wales were triumphant with Meredith scoring one of their goals. Unfortunately the authorities did not recognise the fixture as a "Full" International – much to the disgust of Meredith. However, when he was finally part of a successful Welsh team that 'legitimately' triumphed 1-0 over England the following year, he proclaimed: "Oh, that I have lived to see this day!" The comparison with the plight of modern wing genius Ryan Giggs (yet to qualify for any of the nine major international tournaments which have taken place since his debut in 1991) is clear to see.

Not that the lack of success stopped Meredith playing for his beloved country – even in friendlies, as most matches were in these formative years of international competition. He had won his first cap against Northern Ireland in Belfast on a Saturday in 1895, then was back in London two days later to face England before travelling back to Manchester to play for City two days after that – the days in-between? Back down the pit. Oh, and then he played against Scotland to round off an incredible seven days for which he was paid the total of £3. No wonder 'Old Skinny' as he was sometimes referred to, would laugh in later years at the suggestion that there was too much football played in modern times. In fact, Meredith dismissed the post-war game as 'sissy stuff' – goodness know what he'd have to say about Sir Alex Ferguson and Arsène Wenger's constant calls for a mid-winter break for their 'over-worked players' - if only they knew!

Wales did draw 1-1 with England to win their first Home International championship in 1906/07 inspired by no less than six former Chirk players including Billy and his younger brother Sam Meredith, of Stoke and Leyton.

That 'legitimate' victory against England was Meredith's last cap at the age of 45 years and 8 months, making him still Britain's oldest international footballer.

It is perhaps a testament to just how physically fit Meredith was that he was able to continue to be so effective or so long. He won trophies with United well into his thirties and was still a hugely influential figure for the Reds and it's not as though his contemporaries were all playing football to a ripe old age. Most retired just before or not long after their 30th birthday, but weighed in against a lower life expectancy back then, this should be too startling a revelation During the 1912/1913 season, however, Meredith was dropped for the first time in his career and was not impressed. The relationship between the club and player soured and his days looked numbered at Old Trafford. With the First World War also interrupting a glittering career, Meredith felt he needed to make up for any lost years and during the war, he guested for Stalybridge Celtic and City – his first love clearly holding a spell over the tough former miner.

Yet, though he was now of middle age, Meredith's business with City was unfinished, and in 1921, at 46, he rejoined the club as player/trainer and he was welcomed back as a long, lost son. He had crossed the divide not once, but twice.

Billy played 25 times without scoring during his first season back, and though his effectiveness had dimmed greatly, he still had the odd move that delighted the watching Hyde Road throngs and was still capable of making a full-back less than half his age look silly. His final appearance at Hyde Road was during a 1-0 win over Newcastle United and he played just one league game during City's final season at the crumbling venue – a 2-0 away loss at West Bromwich Albion, but then appeared twice in the league during the Blues' first season at Maine Road during season 1923/24.

Manager Ernest Magnall called upon Meredith's experience for the latter stages of an exciting FA Cup run and he scored his final goal for the club at Maine Road during a 5-1 third round victory over Brighton and Hove Albion – almost 30 years since he'd scored his first against Newton Heath in a match which still makes him the oldest player to appear in an FA Cup tie. Ironically he made his final appearance against the same team he'd begun his City career – Newcastle United – and what a stage to finish his career on – an FA Cup semi-final at Birmingham City's St Andrews. Incredibly, he was just a few weeks shy of his 50th birthday. Only one player has so far broken Meredith's record for longevity at the very pinnacle of the English game – the incomparable Sir Stanley Matthews – a fellow crowd pleaser and gentleman – who played a First Division game aged 50 years and five days.

Sadly, the Blues lost the semi-final 2-0 and the hopes of thousands that this most magnificent footballer could end his playing days at the only place that would have been fitting of such an amazing career – Wembley Stadium – were dashed. A benefit game in Billy's honour a year later bore gate receipts of £871 as City, symbolically given Meredith's ability to bridge divides, took on a combined Celtic and Rangers side at Maine Road – it was no less than he deserved.

MEREDITH'S ACHIEVEMENTS AND stature in the game rank alongside the great Matthews ("I wish Stan had scored more goals," Meredith once commented). But surely it is Billy and not Stan who is the original godfather of wingplay. Matthews never named Meredith as his inspiration as it is unlikely he ever saw him play, even as a small boy in Stoke, but Meredith's legend was purveyed across the country by the media of the day – newspapers and chit-chat. For Billy's stardom came from his pure talent, from what folk witnessed on the field, the style, the flair, the goals, and the glory. Not from the in depth articles in the Sunday glossies, or from the post-match TV or radio interviews.

Without question, Meredith laid down the template for the stylish attacking wing play City fans have demanded/yearned for in the years since he hung up his boots. Clearly ahead of his time, his unusual style and skill introduced a new brand of football to the supporters, and they are still hungry for more to this day. That is his legacy.

The handful of people who were fortunate enough to see both Meredith and Colin Bell play, maintain that it is, at worst, an equal contest as to who is City's greatest ever footballer. Time may have dimmed his sparkle, but the record books prove that, with a career total of 686 games and 287 goals, the miner from Chirk with a love of playing football and chewing toothpicks, was not only City's first Cult Hero, but probably the Blues' greatest player as well. In fact, in total he made more than 300 appearances for both Manchester clubs – a record that will surely never be topped. Quite an epitaph! He died at his home in Withington, Manchester in April 1958, aged 83 and is still revered in his homeland – to the point that a road leading to his beloved Maine Road was renamed after him. Rightly so. What a genius!

Frank Swift

1932-1949: 376 games, 0 goals

IT HAD BEEN nine years since Frank Swift had retired from football. He'd only ever played league football for Manchester City, had represented his country 19 times and had since moved into a career in journalism. Respected universally in the game, he was an ideal choice to cover important games for the *News of the World*. Players wanted to talk to Frank and the public wanted to read what he had to say. He was one of the chosen few who travelled with Manchester United as they took on Red Star Belgrade in the European Cup and, typically, as the plane laboured to take off from Munich on their ill-fated return journey to Manchester, it was Frank Swift who stood up and cracked a joke. Moments later, on the British European Airways' third attempt at a take-off, the plane overshot the runway, hit a house with its portside wing, veered to its right before hitting another building and bursting into flames. Seven of the famous 'Busby Babes' died as well as 14 other people on board. Though Swift was pulled out from the mangled wreckage alive, he died before reaching hospital. It was a tragic end to a fantastic life.

FRANK SWIFT WAS born and raised in Blackpool and enjoyed being close to the sea and the bracing winds of the Fylde coast. His brother played in goal for Bolton Wanderers and bore a striking resemblance to Frank and he earned his spending money by taking tourists on boat trips. He was a strapping teenager who had represented Blackpool Schoolboys and also played at a more senior level for Blackpool Gasworks, for whom he worked for as a coke-keeper. Feeling he had more in him and better potential than the standard of football he was playing at, he wrote a letter to local side Fleetwood Town asking if he might have a trial. He received a note back a few days later with the message: 'You're playing for us Saturday. Don't forget your boots.'

He played for Fleetwood for a while before a friend suggested he write to a bigger club if he felt he could play at a higher level, and that's exactly what he did. City invited him to Maine Road and he played a few times as an amateur in a number of friendly games. Swift had chosen his time well, with no outstanding keeper on the books at the club at the time, the Blues were looking for a youngster they could groom to be the custodian for years to come. It was immediately clear that he was quite a talent, though understandably raw and in need of a little refining. On 21 October 1932, City paid Fleetwood the princely sum of ten shillings (50p) for Swift's services – and that would be his weekly wage for his first year at the club. He travelled with City to watch the Blues go down 3-0 to Everton in the 1933 FA Cup final and just over a year later, and following an 8-0 defeat at Wolves, Swift was given his debut away to Derby County. It was Christmas Day 1933 and the 19-year-old was impressive despite the 4-1 scoreline. The next day, he played against the same opposition and kept a clean sheet in a 2-0 win in front of a 57,218 Boxing Day crowd – it was also his 20th birthday – not a bad way to celebrate.

The fans seemed to take to Swift straight away, with his athleticism and frame seemingly filling the goal. He'd also picked a fine time to come into the team who were about to embark on a triumphant FA Cup run. The Blues had lost the final the year before, going down 3-0 to Everton, but skipper Sam Cowan had told King George V that he would return the following year as the winning captain. The whole team was completely focused on making that bold prediction come true and every player believed it was possible.

Swift had come into a side packed with crowd favourites with the likes of Cowan, Fred Tilson, Eric Brook, Matt Busby, Alec Herd and Ernie Toseland, but there was something special about a goalkeeper whose bravery and courage shone through every time he pulled on the green jersey. Youngsters especially had a new hero to worship and an autograph from Big Frank was a treasured possession, particularly if it gave them a chance to look at his giant hands – a 14-inch span meant that he could grab the ball single-handedly. He was the missing jigsaw for manager Wilf Wild's team who were an excellent cup side having being finalists and semi-finalists in the past two years. As City progressed through the rounds of the 1933/34 season, the crowds flocked to see if the Blues could go all the way to Wembley again. They accounted for Blackburn, Hull City, Sheffield Wednesday (the latter two after a replay) and Stoke City – the latter being played in front of a record provincial crowd of 84,568. Eric Brook's goal set-up yet another semi-final – City's third in succession – this time against Aston Villa. The Birmingham side were favourites for the cup, but it would be an unforgettable day for City who went ahead through Ernie Toseland in the fourth minute and then scored three more in an incredible four minute spell to lead 4-0 at the break. Yet the Blues were hugely indebted to Swift, who'd made two magnificent saves with the score at 1-0. City won the semi-final 6-1 – the biggest win at that stage since 1908 – to earn a place in the final against Portsmouth.

Swift was living his boyhood dream and the final would be unforgettable for many reasons. The Blues dominated the first half yet still fell behind when Rutherford's low drive sped past Swift who touched it on the way into the net. The big keeper, never one to shirk his responsibilities told his team-mates that he might have kept the shot out had he been wearing his gloves. He'd taken the lead from his opposing number who, during a heavy shower, had taken his gloves off. Fred Tilson put his arm round the youngster's shoulder and said in his heavy Yorkshire accent: "Tha don't need to worry. I'll plonk in two in the next half." Tilson duly obliged and scored in the 75th and 78th minutes to clinch the cup for City but the drama wasn't quite over for Swift who had been chatting with photographers about how long was left when, on hearing the final whistle, turned to collect his cap and gloves before collapsing in a heap – he'd fainted.

The physio's smelling salts quickly brought him round and his first words were: "Did we win?" He then sprinted after his team-mates just in time to join on at the back as they climbed the steps to collect the trophy and winners' medals. He later said: "Fancy a great strapping fellow like me fainting in front of all those people and the King."

George V later sent a telegram to enquire about Swift's recovery and Frank wold later explain that the pressure and excitement had simply proved too much for him. That he had admirers in high places should come as no surprise. The great Sunderland skipper Raich Carter said of Swift: "He looks so big in goal that as a forward it often seemed that trying to score against him was like trying to put the ball into a matchbox."

Swift would miss just one game in the next five seasons before the intervention of World War Two – an incredible record and one that one him a legion of admirers among the City faithful. His agility was incredible and he was, at that point, undoubtedly one of the best in the world and it was Swift's innovative long throws up field that introduced a new method for keepers up and down the country and gained him yet further prominence. It was also due to the restricted steps law that was introduced, meaning keepers couldn't run around their box as they had done in the past. Swift, however, had an answer for everything. When faced with a forward standing in front of him to encourage him to take extra steps, would simply throw the ball up and over the player's head, thus regaining his full allocation of legal steps!

In fact, the only player who could genuinely challenge Swift's position as crowd favourite, was new signing Peter Doherty, an Irish international who, ironically, joined from his hometown club Blackpool.

Doherty began life with Coleraine and then joined Glentoran, scoring two goals on his debut for the latter after previously working as a bricklayer and a bus conductor. An outstanding inside-right, he was spotted by Blackpool who paid just £2,000 for his services.

Doherty began his league career with Blackpool around the same time Swift was signing for City, and he would go on to score 29 goals in 89 appearances for the Seasiders. Wilf Wild had been searching for a versatile inside forward that he felt could turn his side into league champions and in Doherty, he'd found his ideal player. When Blackpool's main guarantor Sir Lindsay Parkinson died unexpectedly, it meant Blackpool had to sell some of their brightest stars in order to survive. City seized their chance and put in an offer just shy of £10,000 for Doherty which the Bloomfield Road club reluctantly accepted and he signed on 19 February 1936, making his debut in a 3-1 home defeat to Preston. Doherty must have wondered what he'd let himself in for as North End right-half Bill Shankly followed his every move muttering: "A great wee team North End, a great wee team." Shankly's psychological superiority was clearly showing itself at a very early stage!

The following season, the man christened 'The Prince of Inside Forwards' was in majestic form, scoring 30 goals in 41 appearances as the Blues swept aside all comers to land their first league title ever. Doherty was a majestic sight and worked tirelessly up and down the pitch, challenging, creating and scoring goals as the Blues – he was an instant hero, particularly for the younger supporters who had another idol to cheer on.

The entire side achieved immortality that season and with Swift at one end keeping them out and Doherty at the other end knocking them, the Blues were worthy champions. Yet neither crowd hero could prevent a disastrous campaign as defending champions when Manchester City became the first team to be relegated as title-holders – presumably, this is where the origins of 'typical City' come from! Doherty and Swift were too good to play Second Division football and the graceful Irishman made murmurings that the football at that level was not suiting his game at all and several clubs expressed a strong interest, but the club were not prepared to let him go. Swift, on the other hand came into work, did his job and went home and it was his attitude and loyalty that just edges the Cult Hero status between the pair.

Swift was a one-club man and he loved representing Manchester City and despite failing to win promotion at the first attempt, he was quite happy with his lot. On one occasion, when travelling with his friend, journalist Eric Thornton, he was dashing for a train that was about to pull out.

A young boy in torn clothing and looking in need of a good meal shouted: "Give us your autograph Mr Swift." Risking missing his train, the gentle giant rushed over and scribbled on the boy's pad before ruffling his hair and dashing on his way. The boy looked down at his pad and then a broad smile passed over his face. It later transpired he'd written 'Best of luck to my old pal, Frank Swift'. The boy may have had a tough time, but he'd have a great story to tell his school friends the next day and it was going the extra yard that set Swift apart from others.

The onset of the war meant the cessation of league football and Swift became a special constable in charge of traffic control, but he lasted just a day before returning to City to play 150 times for the club between 1939 and 1945. When the war ended he was ready to begin his league career again with the Blues in earnest but Doherty was set for pastures new, mainly due to an incident that stewed with him for quite some time.

City had a match with Crewe at Gresty Road and it was at a time when few clubs knew what their line-ups would be until just before kick-off because players serving in the armed forces would need to obtain a 24-hour pass from their commanding officers. It meant that many of the team were left facing a race against time to get to the venue and if they were late, it was their hard luck because it was a case of no play, no pay.

Doherty was down to play but faced a gruelling cross-country trek to get to Crewe, but he was determined that distance should not prevent him leading the line for the Blues. He left his barracks first on foot, then by bus and then by hitching the remaining miles on a coal truck! He just managed to make it with about 20 minutes to spare but the team had stripped and was ready for action – and the twelfth man had been given Doherty's shirt. The club officials told Doherty they wouldn't be changing the line-up and told him his journey had been wasted. He accepted their decision with good grace, but inwardly, he was seething and knew in his heart that he would never play league football for the Blues again.

To compound the situation, with players allowed to guest for other clubs during that period, Doherty turned out several times for Derby, but when the Rams asked if they could play him in the FA Cup, City refused and he had to sit out the competition completely. If it wasn't bad enough that he'd been forced to lose the best years of his career to the war, the refusal to let him play on the odd occasions he could manage it left him cold.

But, his attitude was 'If you can't say anything good about someone, say nothing at all.' As it was, his actions spoke louder than words and when football began again following the war, he slapped in a transfer request. He would never play for City again and joined Derby County on 6 December 1945.

Swift had served his time in the armed forces and there was one occasion that was almost a portent of the tragic events of 1958. While travelling in an RAF Dakota over France in 1944, the plane was involved in a near-miss. That his former City team-mate Matt Busby was also aboard this aircraft is quite incredible considering that both these individuals were to be involved in the Munich crash, fatally in Frank's case.

Meanwhile, continued from where he had left off and with the added advantage of his old mate Sam Cowan taking charge from November onwards, a new-look City side began to stamp their authority on the Second Division. They embarked on a 22-match unbeaten run that would see them comfortably take the Second Division league title. The country was still in the throes of recovering from an exhausting conflict with Germany and football was a welcome relief from poverty and, in some cases, desolation.

City had offered to share their ground with Manchester United, with Old Trafford have being bombed during the war and Swift on occasion said he might fancy playing for 'the other lot' across the road. There was, however, no way club officials would ever allow that and when United made an official enquiry in October 1946, it was flatly rejected.

Many people, it seemed, had a funny story to tell about 'Big Frank' who was always available for supporters wanting autographs and suchlike. On one occasion, a small boy asked him for his signature and the awe-struck kid asked his hero how he could also become a great goalkeeper. "Well son," said Swift, "after every match in which a goal has been scored against me, I make a practice of sitting down and drawing diagrams to see if I was at fault."

A few weeks later, following an 8-2 defeat by Bradford City in the FA Cup, Swift came across the same boy waiting on the same street as before. "Do you want my autograph again, son?" he asked.

"No," replied the boy. "I just came to tell you that you've got a lot of homework to do this evening." Though Swift took losing badly, he couldn't help breaking out in laughter. The kids loved how he'd walk out of the tunnel carrying a ball in one hand and it just added to the man-mountain myth he'd earned.

On another occasion, City were playing against Liverpool at Anfield. It was shortly after the war and food rationing was still the norm. Swift produced a breathtaking save right in front of the Kop and the appreciative Liverpool supporters were so impressed that they threw dozens of oranges at him! The delighted Swift quickly gathered them up and stored in the back of the goal ready to take home with him later.

The stories regarding Big Frank come thick and fast and there was another occasion when he was travelling on a public bus after a home game, and the guy who was sitting next to him moaned throughout the whole trip about the awful City keeper without actually recognising that he was sat next to him!

Swift's form earned him a first full cap against Northern Ireland on 28 September 1946 and one can only imagine how many he might have won had it not been for the war, though he had made 14 appearances for his country during the conflict. This however, had been his first 'official' appearance.

A week earlier, he was in goal for City at West Ham on 5 October 1946 and during the second half was joshing with the home fans about The Hammers' inability to score – even though City hadn't scored either. As the game edged towards a goalless draw, West Ham won a throw in on the left. The ball was touched on to Archie Macaulay who rose and planted the ball into the net. The Hammers' fans went mad and Swift knew there'd be a lot of stick to take. He took it all in a good spirit, grinned and called out "fluke" as he got the ball out of the net.

Swift would go on to win 19 caps in all – still scant reward for one of the best goalkeepers this country has ever seen. He earned his second cap just two days later and England would lose just two of the 19 games Swift played in.

On 16 May 1948, Swift entered the record books after he became the first goalkeeper to captain England since Alexander Morten in 1873 when they took on – and beat – Italy 4-0 in Turin. He was 36 by this point and he was considering a life outside the game, though he played one more full season for the

Blues before announcing his retirement. He began the 1948/49 season by conceding a goal after just seven seconds. Preston kicked off and the ball was played out to winger Bobby Langton who looked up and fired in a shot as Swift was throwing his cap and gloves into the net in preparation for the match ahead. City eventually won 302 and Swift's form throughout the season was imperious, with some even suggesting he was in the form of his life.

The club were disappointed, then, to lose such a vital part of their team, especially as he was physically fit and in great shape. In lieu of his fantastic service, they went along with his decision, though a serious illness to reserve keeper Alec Thurlow, left the club thin on the ground for keepers an Swift returned to play four more games for City before hanging his boots up for the final time following a 0-0 draw with Everton at Maine Road on 7 September 1949.

Matt Busby would again try to sign Swift and wanted to bring him out of retirement, such was his reputation, but City, perhaps a little selfishly, balked the approach and held the keeper's registration until 1955, six years after he'd finished playing. It's clear that the club never wanted him to play for anybody else and went to great lengths to ensure that was the case.

With 376 appearances in league and cup games for the Blues, plus a further 133 starts in wartime games for the club (plus one for Hamilton Academicals), Frank Swift clocked up more than 500 appearances for City over a 17-year-period. Jovial and full of life, his presence would light up any gathering and would always hold his hands up when he knew he was in the wrong.

Close friends said Swift found not playing football week in, week out much harder to deal with than he'd anticipated and he missed life at Maine Road, the roar of the crowd and the adulation heaped on him by the City supporters – who wouldn't? But he eventually found other ways to occupy his time, becoming a director in a Moss Side-based cleaning company and then beginning a life in journalism, ultimately for the Sunday best-selling *News of the World*. Of course, this new career path would also lead to his tragic death, but chances are if Frank Swift could have chosen to have died still being involved in football, he'd have grasped it with the two safe hands that served him so well for almost two decades.

Larger than life and a truly talented goalkeeper, it's no wonder Frank Swift was a Cult Hero for the Manchester City fans that clearly adored him. Sadly, when a minority of supporters sing about the Munich Air Disaster, they seem to have either forgotten or are ignorant of what this great man meant to Manchester City.

His replacement would be a little-known German keeper playing for St Helens. Whoever he was, he had giant shoes to fill…

To end, however, there should be one final story that perfectly sums up the spirit that Frank Swift played the game in and lived life to. City were away to Sunderland who were awarded a penalty. The great Len Shackleton, a controversial but hugely entertaining figure himself, decided to take the kick and retreated to the halfway line for his run up. Shack raced in, but at the last moment, with Big Frank already committed to dive one way, Shackleton stopped and gently back-heeled the ball into the empty half of the net. As the players returned to line up for the restart Swift charged after 'Shack', grabbed him by the head and landed a big kiss on his forehead. When will you see anything like that again?

Bert Trautmann

1949-1964: 545 games, 0 goals

THE PAUL NEWMAN movie *Somebody Up There Likes Me* could never be confused with the life story of Bernd – 'Bert' to everyone in England - Trautmann. A mixture of courage beyond the boundaries of even the bravest men, heroism and tragedy – it's been an incredible life for the former German PoW. But if one month in particular could sum up the peaks and troughs of this amazing man's life, it was May 1956. Trautmann's heroics at Wembley will never be forgotten and have been well told and passed on over the years. For the record, City led 3-1 against Birmingham City and just needed to see the game out when Birmingham's Murphy raced through to challenge City keeper Trautmann for the 50/50 ball. The clash left Trautmann, who held the ball, in agony. He suffered excruciating pain in his neck but, after the token treatment that could be offered, he insisted he finish the game – there was the FA Cup at stake, let's not forget. The City defence rallied – the whole team surrounded their No.1 as though their lives depended on it – Bert's probably really did – and they kept Birmingham at bay. Trautmann received more treatment before collecting his winner's medal from the Queen. Three weeks later, with the Press still lauding his incredible bravery, his son wandered on to a busy road near a friend's home and was killed. John Michael Trautmann was just six-years-old. His father, with a broken neck diagnosed by this time, had flown to Germany as guest of his homeland's FA for a match with England. He returned home immediately, probably wondering what he'd done to deserve this latest and most severe blow.

IT SAYS MUCH about Manchester City Football Club that they would even consider taking on a former German paratrooper just four years after the war. The conflict had lasted seven years and millions of people had died as Hitler attempted to make Europe his own and despite the brief passage of time, feelings ran high as virtually every family had either lost family or their home between 1938 and 1945. But that's what the club did; they needed a larger-than-life figue to replace Frank Swift and Bert Trautmann, a PoW that had been allowed to stay in England after the war finished, who had shown his capabilities as a goalkeeper for St Helens Town, was signed on. To say the decision caused uproar would be something of an understatement. But sign him they did and some 17 years later, when he reluctantly retired from the game, he could look back with pride and a breathtaking career.

Trautmann had served three years in the Wehrmacht when he was captured by the English, whose first words, claimed Bert, were, "Hello Fritz, fancy a cup of tea?" After the Normandy landings he was brought back to England as a prisoner. In fact, he had been caught three times before, by the Russians, Free French and the Americans. There were various camps all over England, but Bert's was Prison Camp 50, near in Ashton-in –Makerfield, not far from Haydock racecourse, enabling him to take part in the sporting events he'd loved as a young man in his home town of Ruedesheim where he excelled in track and field . It was no holiday camp, but the prisoners were treated fairly and Bert enjoyed a match every now in a thriving league set up by the

German prisoners, and then, playing in his usual role as a centre-half he picked up an injury and asked goalkeeper Gunther Luhr if he'd swap positions – which he did – and he went in goal for the remainder of the game. A few decent saves later and the former paratrooper discovered he actually liked throwing himself around in goal – his parachute jump training meant he was quite adept at landing on the ground without injuring himself. The prisoners were allowed limited freedom and it was during such time that Bert met a local girl called Margaret and they soon fell in love and were married. With the war over, Bert decided to make his home in England and he volunteered to stay one year and began to turn out for local Liverpool Combination side St Helens Town – his performances soon had scouts from several clubs interested and though he had several offers from top clubs, he always politely said no, adding he was happy where he was. The crowds at St Helens went from 250 to almost 6,000 as word spread of the "amazing German goalkeeper". When Manchester City offered him a contract however, he decided to accept, and signed the appropraite forms while in bed with flu and the clock reading 11.56pm when manager Jock Thomson and director Robert Smith left for Manchester.

Before he left, the players, officials and supporters presented Bert with a hamper, packed with tinned food, ham, butter, sugar and an envelope stuffed with fifty £1 notes. The people of St Helens had used their own food rations to help his family in Germany and it reduced the strapping six-footer to tears. It was also an early indicator of how people would treat Bert once they got to know him for who he was, not what they thought he represented.

When the news broke that City had signed a German, an almighty war of attrition broke out between the live-and-let-live section of supporters and those who just couldn't forgive the fact he'd fought against their country just a few years earlier. The questions those who opposed the signing were asking were on an emotional level but not without justification – had this man killed a member of their family? Who would know? Feelings ran high, particularly in Manchester's Jewish community, who saw the blond, blue-eyed Aryan as the living embodiment of everything Hitler had held as physical perfection, and protestations would continue for several years. There were, however, a large proportion of fans who wanted to get on with their lives and leave the war behind as best they could.

"I was told 20 to 40,000 people took to the streets in protest," said Bert.

Boycotts were threatened, but Bert showed a characterstic that would remain with him throughout his life – that of integrity. He was a decent man who had done what he'd had to do, like millions of other soldiers. He hadn't wanted to spend years fighting men he didn't even know, but he had no choice. Now it was over and it was time to move on – if he could remain in 'enemy territory' and elect to build a new life with the people of England, he at least deserved the chance to be allowed to try.

Before his first match for City, Bert said: "I invite those who object to meet me in Manchester and we can talk it over because I have always looked upon sport as a means of bringing people together."

D-Day sergeant and City skipper at the time Eric Westwood personally welcomed him to Maine Road before the rest of the team hoisted him on their shoulders for a picture. "The war's over now, " he told waiting reporters, "and he comes to us a s a player, not a Hitler soldier. We welcome him." At the first training session, Thomson organised Westwood, Ronnie Turnbull and Dennis Westcott to take shots on Bert so they could see what he was made of. Each player fired in a powerful shot, one of which was palmed round the post and the other two caught. After half-an-hour, Westwood had seen enough. "We've got a great goalkeeper here, and that's been proved up to the hilt," he said. "He's one of the greatest I've ever seen."

A much larger crowd than usual turned out to watch Bert's first game for City – a reserve match against Barnsley where it quickly became obvious that he was a very good keeper. A few more stunning displays for the second string and Thomson decided Trautmann was ready for the first team and he was selected to play against Bolton Wanderers at Burnden Park. He was jeered by some, but he rode them out and made some good saves, though he couldn't prevent a 3-0 defeat.

He was coming into a City team that was clearly struggling for its First Division life but was just grateful to be playing at the highest level in England. Yet it was not only the fact that he was an ex-German PoW, he was also filling the sizeable boots of Frank Swift, a god-like figure to the Manchester City fans. Alec Thurlow had been lined up to replace Swift but fell ill and would later die, still a young man.

Trautmann made his home debut on 26 November 1949 in front of 30,501 fans at Maine Road and if he'd been nervous, who could blame him? But it didn't show. He kept a clean sheet in a 4-0 win over Birmingham City, but it was merely the calm before the storm as his next game saw Derby County put seven past him without the Blues replying. But though each away game brought its share of hecklers, the dissentors at Maine Road were becoming noticeably less each game.

Trautmann had so many plusses to his game. Excellent in one-on-one situations, a master of plucking crosses out of the air and a wonderful thrower of the ball. Years of practice of throwing while he was a youngster in Bremen meant he was accurate and could launch the ball long distances. "I played handball and volleyball as a young man and I could throw the ball some distance with great accuracy. I could make it swerve or do anything I wanted," he said.

Trautmann had also studied some of the game's great keepers – names such as Jack Fairbrother of Preston, Ted Sagar of Everton and his hero, Frank Swift, perhaps the reason he chose City over a dozen other clubs. The remainder of the 1949/50 season saw his fan club grow in numbers but City relegated. Without Trautmann, the Blues' fate would have been sealed far sooner but there was optimism the hiatus didn't have to be more than a year.

Trautmann and his wife holidayed in Bremen, where he'd often suffered homesickness for, but after intending a 12-week summer stay, after five weeks Bert said to his wife, "Pack the bags, luv and let's go home." It was a pivotal point in Bert's life and the realisation that Hazel Grove was now his home was not an upsetting one.

While Margaret struggled to buy presents to take home, Bert spoke to the salesman and explained what she was trying to say. The salesman replied, "I say, sir, for an Englishman, you speak excellent German." Bert smiled, not quite sure why that statement was so comforting.

But Bert's first season with City had been an explosive one. Ex-servicemen vowed never to follow the club again, season-tickets were torn up, shop windows smashed and fights even broke out on the terraces as supporters argued among themselves. He'd won some of them over, but not all.

Now to the meat of the matter. How, I hear you protest, can a club legend like Trautmann end up in a list of 20 Cult Heroes? Well, of course, he became a club legend and in the following pages I shall explain exactly why. But, for this writer, anyway, to be a Cult Hero there has to be something that has divided opinion. If the player has had to win over a few fans to become a legend, fine, he belongs in a book on legends. If a player has had to win over a large number of fans, he's on the right lines to be in this book – though every entry is included for differing reasons, Bert Trautmann had so many disadvantages stacked against him that if he can't be considered a Cult Hero, I'm not sure who can. He didn't have to just win a few hundred of his own fans over, he had a whole nation to contend against – and he won – hands down, so to speak.

Each week, the jeers became less and the cheers became louder. A hero was being born before the City fans' eyes and the move to sign him, described by some as "crass stupidity" was perhaps the first real bridge between England and Germany since VE-Day. Oh, and aside from all the political shenanigans, City had signed a wonderful player. Les McDowall replaced Jock Thomson as manager and began to build a team around Trautmann, who would play every game as City were promoted as runners-up at the first attempt. The following year, he missed just one game but there was one game that would remain in the memories of those who were in attendance for most of their lives. City travelled to Tottenham on 6 October 1951 to play against a team that had English football's largest Jewish fan-base. It was a potentially explosive afternoon and it began with the majority of the massive 57,550 crowd jeering, hissing and abusing Trautmann. A true professional, Trautmann played the game and turned in a brilliant display to help City to a 2-1 win. As he left, spontaneous and thunderous applause broke out from thousands of Spurs fans who recognised the courage of the City keeper, and, of course, his brilliance.

The next two seasons, Bert was an ever-present and he seemed invincible, especially to the kids who idolised him unconditionally. By this time, 1954, he'd built up a huge fan-base around the country and at City, he was simply irreplaceable.

He was in goal when City took on – and lost to – Newcastle United in the 1955 FA Cup final, but there was little he could do as the Geordies powered their way to a 3-1 win. Like Sam Cowan before him, City skipper Roy Paul promised his team would return as victors the following year, but even the Welsh man-mountain couldn't have imagined quite how controversial the path and the final itself it would be.

Trautmann was seen as the villain by Tottenham fans after a semi-final victory for City appeared to be sealed by Trautmann holding the leg of a Spurs striker in the closing seconds of the game. Many sent poison-pen letters to Trautmann telling him to go home, and, not surprisingly, much worse. Their beef was he'd cheated their team out of a draw and Bert passed the letters, all anonymous, to the police. He said: "They are very upsetting, but I am trying to forget all about them."

Any doubts about Bert's integrity would dissolve forever in the space of 90 minutes just two months later as City walked out to face Birmingham City in the 1956 FA Cup final. Trautmann dived at the feet of centre-forward Peter Murphy, taking the ball before rolling over and lying still. When Trautmann lay hurt, you knew it was genuine because it had virtually never happened before. At last, he got to his feet, a little shakily, and made his way back to his goal rubbing his neck, his vision blurred.

After what seemed like an eternity, the whistle blew for time and City had won the cup. Bert took his place with the rest of his team-mates and Bill Leivers helped him up the stairs to collect his medal, but a few days later, he was told by doctors at the Manchester Royal Infirmary that he was lucky to be alive. He'd badly broken a vertebrae and several others had been displaced. His life had literally hung by a thread and as news spread of his amazing courage, any doubters were levelled in one fell swoop – this was a man who bordered on super-human. Protests, death threats, hate mail and even a broken neck – nothing could stop him and within six months he was once again donning the green jersey as Manchester City's goalkeeper. It was *Boy's Own* stuff and then some. He had not only become the first German to collect a winner's medal at Wembley, he became the first foreign recipient of the much-coveted Football Writers' Player of the Year award the same year.

By this time, he was an honorary Englishman and he proved as much when, in 1959, City played a friendly in Germany against a local side, Tasmania. City won 2-1, but Trautmann was disgusted with the way his countrymen had treated his team-mates and in particular Billy McAdams, who was sent off for an innocuous looking challenge. "We'll never play here again," he said. "I am disgusted. I cannot speak for the team but this is very upsetting. I was in the Olympic Stadium as a boy and I always looked forward to playing international sport there and bettering the relations between our two countries. But this sort of thing sickens me.

How my team-mates managed to restrain themselves, I don't know. All credit to them. The Germans just don't realise how much harm they are doing themselves."

A year later came one of his proudest moments, when he was selected to play for a Football League side to face an Irish League XI – as captain – the first time a goalkeeper had ever been asked to lead the team since Frank Swift, who had recently died in the Munich Air Disaster, in Turin 12 years earlier. What a magnificent coup for Manchester City and yet further testament to how Bert had become ingrained into the nation's psyche.

The late fifties and early sixties had proved a barren time for City and they flirted with relegation for many years, missing by the skin of their teeth on several occasions, but Trautmann did his best to keep the club afloat with his usual batch of unbelieveable saves, breathtaking bravery and all-round excellence in goal. But he was frustrated with being beaten so many times as the team struggled to keep their heads above water and his anger showed with a series of uncharacteristic tantrums resulting in a sending off and suspensions for various disrepute charges.

The years were taking their toll, though and part-way through the 1962/63 campaign, he was dropped in favour of youngster Harry Dowd – City were relegated that year, and the following season, aged 39, Trautmann played just three more games before announcing his intention to retire from the game. With 545 appearance for the Blues, he was safely ensconced in the club's all-time greats, and Sir Stanley Matthews rated Bert as the best keeper he'd ever seen. He played his last game for the Blues on 28 March 1964 during a 2-0 defeat at Preston North End.

City rewarded Trautmann with a testimonial a few weeks later on 15 April – it would be perhaps the greatest testimonial this country had ever seen, before or since with a host of world famous British talent desperate to be part of an unforgettable evening. A combined City and United side were to take on an International XI and the sides lined up thus: Trautmann, Lievers, Cantwell, Setters, Foulkes, Oakes, Murray, Kevan, Charlton, Law, Wagstaffe. The International team was: Springett, Armfield, Wilson, Clayton, Miller, Adamason, Matthews, Quixall, Johnstone, Connelly. This was an opportunity for the Manchester City fans to say a heart-felt thanks to the big German who'd won their respect and ultimately their hearts.

Fans queued for hours to get into the stadium and some would be disappointed. Estimates for the crowd are sketchy, but it's likely 60,000 people squeezed into the ground that night, all there to bid farewell to one of the game's greatest characters and one of the best goalkeepers – if not the best – the world had ever seen. To illustrate just how extraordinary that crowd was, just 8,054 fans had attended the home game with Middlesbrough just a month earlier and it was likely the biggest gate at Maine Road for four years.

The players played their hearts out but the game would never finish as, with three minutes remaining, thousands of Trautmann admirers couldn't restrain themselves any longer and they swarmed on to the pitch, mobbing Trautmann in an emotional outpouring rarely seen in post-war England. Police eventually escorted the overwhelmed keeper to the safety of the dressing rooms, as "Trautmann! Trautmann! Trautmann!" echoed around Maine Road. It was the biggest crowd of the season. Bert, tears streaming down his face, returned to announce over a microphone, "This is the greatest moment of my life." The roars rendered further words pointless. Crowds gathered outside the main entrance to sing "For He's A Jolly Good Fellow" and even the photographers had had a whipround and presented Bert with a cigarette lighter. That night will stay with Bert, now in his eighties, for as long as he lives.

Though verbally promised a job for life, Bert wasn't found one and his post-playing career was littered with jobs that were, frankly, beneath him and it is mystifying why the club couldn't invent a role for one of their favourite sons

Years after his retirement, he took part in Johnny Hart's testimonial and was once again lauded by the City supporters, many who suggested he would be a better option at almost 50 than the out-of-sorts Joe Corrigan. He eventually left England and at the time of writing, spent most of the year in Valencia and the rest of the time in Germany. In 2004 he was awarded the OBE by the Queen and also inducted into the Manchester City Hall of Fame.

"As a goalkeeper, you have to dive 15,000 times in your career," he said in a recent interview. "The warm sun in Spain helps the ache and pains," he added. If Bert is any nationality, he is Germglish, or Engman – he is the embodiment of two nations that are separated by their similarities. "If I'm in England and people criticise Germany, I defend Germany. If I'm in Germany and people criticise England, I defend England. If I could afford to live in England, I would because the people are so wonderful. Bremen is my birthplace," he adds, "but Manchester is my home and I thank everyone for their acceptance, hospitality and friendship."

Manchester is a place Bert will always be welcome – particularly as he is one of the greatest players to ever don the City shirt and, I hope you'll by this point agree, a genuine Cult Hero.

Roy Paul

1950-1957: 293 games, 17 goals

DEFEATED CAPTAIN SAM Cowan promised to take Manchester City back to Wembley the following year after his side were beaten in the 1933 FA Cup final. He was true to his word and the Blues returned to win in 1934, inspired by their captain. Just 21 years later, City skipper Roy Paul trudged down the steps at Wembley after a 3-1 defeat to Newcastle United. He had given his loser's medal away within a few minutes because he didn't want to be associated with losing anything, especially the greatest club match in the world, but he vowed to return the next year, just as Cowan had done, and lift the FA Cup as the winning captain. "I think we'll have another crack at this," he told his crestfallen team-mates. "We shall be here again next year and if we don't win, you'll have me to reckon with." When it came to inspirational skippers, Roy Paul knew a thing or to. City did return a year later and Paul was the proudest man in Britain as he lifted the famous old trophy above his head. Sadly, this was as good as it got for the Welsh legend, but his life, career and attitude was a mixture of exotic highs, laughter and lows and even to this day, Paul is regarded as perhaps the club's greatest ever captain – if not the best, certainly the most inspirational...

GELLI PENTRE LIES in the middle of the dramatic South Wales landscape that is collectively known as the Rhondda Valley. Some 20 miles from Cardiff, the lifeblood of the villages and towns along the valley was mining and back in the 1920s and 30s there was little else to do but work and go down to the local for a few beers. Hard workers and hard drinkers – that was the culture of the menfolk who were as tough as the coal faces they mined.

But the little-known outpost of Gelli Pentre would be the birthplace of one of the country's most fascinating characters and a footballer who today should be remembered alongside the likes of Welsh heroes like John Charles and Billy Meredith – that he isn't is more to do with what happened after his career, but we'll come to that later.

The future for the young Roy Paul was no different from that of his father and his father before. A life down the pits beckoned, as it did for every young boy, but the youngster showed a flair for football from an early age and by 12 he was playing for a local men's side on slack-coal pitches and as a teenager, he was signed on by Swansea Town – his express ticket away from a life down the pit. He soon earned a reputation as one of the toughest wing-halves in the country and, but the outbreak of war in 1939, his path to fame and fortune would have been cleared far sooner.

At Swansea he'd served a brutal apprenticeship under the watchful eye of coach Frank Barson who might just possibly be the dirtiest play to have ever lived. So fearsome was his reputation that opposing players would visibly wilt at the sight of mad dog Barson steaming towards them intent on inflicting pain, broken bones or worse. 'Dirty Frank', who had so many enemies it was rumoured he carried a knife and a gun wherever he went, had seen something in Paul that he believed he could develop – a streak of granite that might take him to the very top. He began to impress on him every trick in the book and Paul and Swansea soon reaped the benefit.

One thing nobody had to teach Paul was the gift of the gab and when he volunteered for national service, he convinced the powers-that-be that he would be best utilised as a swimming instructor in the Royal Marines. He got the job despite not being able to swim a single stroke. That was, as they say, Roy Paul all over. He returned home to work in the mines for a short time and when the war ended, Paul had developed a wanderlust that needed satisfying. He made his international debut for Wales against England, but he wanted more out of life. Paid a pittance for playing the game he loved, when several top names were lured to South America on the promise of riches beyond their wildest dreams, Paul decided he wanted a taste of the high-life, too. He met with Jock Dodds, an agent for several South American clubs and after leaving his wife Beryl with a usual kiss on the doorstep, on an impulse he set off for a new chapter of his career abroad, taking with him not so much as a toothbrush or overcoat. He was soon on a flight to Bogota in Colombia – Beryl thought he'd gone to Swansea!

Within a few days, he and his pal and Swansea team-mate Jack Hedley, who'd also found the lure of South American dollars too tempting to turn down, turned up at the aptly-named Millionairis looking forward to his signing-on fee of £4,000 and a monthly wage of £200 – four times his salary in Wales. But the promise of the high-life and luxury apartment soon faded when the Colombian outfit refused to give Hedley a contract because he wasn't an international. Paul didn't much fancy being out there without his drinking buddy and promptly left for home.

'The Bogota Scandal' as it soon became known, saw dozens of players banned from playing in England or Wales again, but when it became clear Paul's move had collapsed before he'd played, he was allowed to carry on playing league football, though a fine of £250 was in effect almost half-a-year's salary at the Vetch Field.

With his horizons broadened and a taste for more money, Paul told Swansea he wouldn't play for them again and, knowing the stubborn man from the Valleys was not likely to change his mind, they reluctantly put their star player on the transfer list. Several top English sides were immediately interested and Manchester United were believed to head the queue – but it was their neighbours Manchester City who stumped up with a record bid of £25,000 - £4,000 more than the previous record paid for Alf Ramsey – and Paul, now aged 31, was on his way to Maine Road.

City had been at their topsy-turvy best since the war, winning promotion as champions in 1947, but relegated just three seasons later. New manager Les McDowall knew his side needed a leader – a fearsome figure who could drag the Blues up by the scruff of their neck, give them a slap around the chops when needed and turn them into something approaching a decent football team. McDowall thought only of Roy Paul and his board backed him to the hilt, so that when he told them 'this is the player who will make the club great again', they understood they couldn't take the chance of letting him slip through their fingers.

The first player to greet Paul was his long-time friend from South Wales, Roy Clarke. Clarke had joined from Third Division Cardiff City in time for the last game of the previous season and the pair were delighted to be reunited.

"When Les McDowall told us he was signing Roy, in all honesty, the players were astounded," recalled Clarke. " To pay a record fee for a 31-year-old seemed madness, but the manager was proved right and the players wrong.

"I met him at the station on his arrival and the first thing I noticed was that he didn't have a bag with him. He told ne he'd left it on the bus from Swansea. It wasn't until months later that his wife told me he'd left Swansea without a thing. I wouldn't have minded but I felt sorry for him and lent him all my good clothes!

"He was an amazing character and his life off the pitch was no secret. He enjoyed himself to the full and didn't try to hide it."

While Paul's boozing during his Maine Road years would become legendary, so would his leadership. He was quite simply a man-mountain and wouldn't allow any shirkers in his team. He was hard as nails, though fair with it. When Paul hit somebody with a crunching tackle, they stayed hit... nobody came back for more.

He made his debut in a 4-2 win at Preston as the Blues began their bid to win promotion to Division One at the first attempt. Wearing the No.6 shirt, City's collosus cajoled, scolded and instructed and the team responded instantly. McDowall, never the most expressive of men, even allowed himself a wry smile as he watched the Welshman inspire those around him.

Unbeaten in 10 games, the Blues had the perfect base to challenge for promotion, and though patchy form in the second half of the campaign almost cost them dearly, City finished runners-up and returned to the top flight after just a one-year absence. He'd missed just one game – a return trip to play Swansea in front of a packed and expectant Vetch Field – perhaps there was an agreement that he should miss this game in view of the controversy surrounding his departure.

Paul was never short of a decent quote and became friendly with a couple of local journalists, Eric Todd and Eric Thornton and after taking a liking to a tie Todd was wearing prior to a match at home to Birmingham City on Christmas Day 1950, he asked Todd if he could have it. Todd replied he could if he managed to score two goals. Not renowned for his scoring prowess, Paul duly powered home two goals during a 3-1 win over Birmingham City and without changing or even visiting the dressing rooms, he sprinted up the steps in the Main Stand and relieved Todd of his tie, which, fortunately for him, he was happy to hand over.

It wasn't a dream return for City, however, and the Blues escaped relegation by the skin of their teeth after losing four of their last five games of the season. There was a slight improvement the following year, but while Paul did his utmost to steady the ship, several of the players around him just weren't up to the task.

It would take the emergence of wing-half Ken Barnes to help galvanise an average side into a good one and the 1954/55 season, with Paul now aged 34, would be the most memorable for a number of years.

The Welshman continued to drink heavily and in later years would say he often played with a heavy hangover or even enjoyed one or two drinks prior to a game! Roy Clarke doubted Paul played while under the influence. He said: "He might have spent the night boozing but you would never know in training. He could run everybody at the club into the ground."

The supporters loved Paul. They loved the fact he was a hard man who didn't take any messing around and they loved the stories of his boozing. Like fellow countryman Billy Meredith some 50 years before, he'd come from the pits and wanted to make the most of his life on the surface and if that meant earning the repuation as something of a hellraiser, then so be it.

Fellow hardman Dave Ewing was a popular figure, too, but the handsome, rugged Paul just had that Roy of the Rovers type aura about him. Fans could relate and chat with the skipper in any of the locals around Maine Road – not something you're likely to see too often these days and not that commonplace back then, either.

Ken Barnes, a colourful character himself, became good friends with Paul and he recalled an incident that pretty much summed up the Welshman: "Roy used to let his hair down after a match and I remember he was particularly merry after a few beers on the coach after an away game.

"In those days, players called the directors 'sir' and jumped when they spoke - but not Roy Paul. He marched up to the chairman Bob Smith and promptly pulled his bowler hat down over his eyes. I don't think the old boy was as amused as everybody else on the coach,"

His tackling was legendary and he was prepared to take the knocks, too. He was fair but firm – except for one occasion that Roy Clarke felt was totally out of character with his game. Said Clarke: "He must have been the hardest tackler in the game at that time, although he was usually very fair. The only time I can really recall him really having a go at another player was when we played QPR in the Second Division, not long after he'd joined.

"He went over the ball to their inside-right and there was a loud 'crack' that you could hear all over the ground. While they sent for the stretcher, I told Roy he was a dirty so-and-so for doing that. He just looked at me and said: 'I have never once complained or retaliated after being fouled, but I have been waiting for three years to get my own back on that fellow and my turn came today. I have never put a fist up to another player, never threatened another player and never said I was sorry to another player. I don't intend to change now.'"

Another reason for Paul's popularity was his refusal to bow down to others. He did his own thing and if others didn't like it, that was there problem. During a presentation dinner at a local football club, Paul went missing. Journalist Eric Todd, who'd been sitting next to him, went to see if he could find him. The City skipper was discovered in the cellar of the pub the dinner was being held in and he'd obviously taken a liking to the local brew!

Todd recalled: "I drove Roy home to Chorlton and the last I saw of him was him careering down the middle of the road with a huge basket of fruit on his head – part of his fee for the evening and he was doing a passable impersonation of Carmen Miranda."

City finished seventh in 54/55 but went all the way to Wembley only to lose to Newcastle United 3-1. It had been a tough path to the Twin Towers and Paul was disconsolate after the defeat. After he'd bathed and changed, he saw his journalist friend Eric Thornton and asked if he wanted the loser's medal he'd received not an hour before from the Queen.

"Do you want this medal, Eric?" he asked. "I've no time for a loser's medal. I want a winner's medal – that's what I want. When I walk up to the Queen, I want it to be as skipper of a team that's won the cup."

Later, during the close season, Paul saw Thornton and said: "You remember telling me about Sam Cowan taking City back to Wembley after they'd been defeated, and then winning the cup? Well I reckon we're going to do the same."

Thornton said he sincerely hoped he would and Paul smiled and said: "We shall, because I'm going to breathe the idea into them from now on and, anyway, we've got to win it this season because I'm getting a bit older and time's running out."

Paul had chosen the 1956/57 campaign to be his career's crowning glory and it was his determination and belief that would carry the players – and the fans – through some difficult games that season.

It was a cup run filled with drama and controversy, but one that would ultimately see Paul realise his dream. An abandoned tie and a replay saw Blackpool off. A tricky trip to Southend, where a flooded pitch had threatened the tie – only for the chairman to order the pitch be dug up in the middle and tonnes of cockle shells be dumped underneath to help the drainage – saw City triumph 1-0 in knee-high-mud.

Then, after seemingly losing the edge against Liverpool in a 0-0 draw at Maine Road in the fifth round, the Blues took a 2-1 lead. The hosts appeared to have equalised as the referee blew for time – had the ball crossed the line? The Liverpool players furiously protested but Paul had the presence of mind to order his team to sprint off and help make the official's mind up for him! Many believe had he not done that, the ref may have changed his mind. Onlookers agreed the goal should have stood but Roy Paul was on a mission. Everton and Spurs were dispatched – the latter being denied a clear penalty in the semi-final and, just as he'd prophesised, Paul led Manchester City out to take on Birmingham City in the 1956 FA Cup final.

This time City went ahead early on and were 3-1 midway through the second half. In a team of heroes, Bert Trautmann was injured when a Birmingham forward's knee slammed into his neck. He played on with a broken neck and City won 3-1 – the pride on Paul's face said it all and he proudly held the FA Cup aloft and savoured the moment. At 36-years-old, he was entitled to give himself a pat on the back – he'd achieved what he'd always set out to do and would be immortalised for making the City fans proud again.

He remained for one more season before the club sanctioned a deal for him to become player-manager of non-league Worcester City. That meant he could move back home to the Rhondda Valley, where his heart had never been far from, and commute from there. But that wasn't the end of Roy Paul, winner of 42 caps for his country. In 1959, aged 39, he inspired the Midland minnows to the third round of the FA Cup, where they drew the mighty Liverpool. The night before the tie, Roy Clarke recalled a phone conversation with his old mate: "He was blind drunk! I could hardly understand a word he was saying. He played the match with the mother of all hangovers but he inspired them to win 2-1 – one of the biggest shocks of all-time."

In fact, Paul claimed to have double-vision during that game, one Worcester City fans still talk about to this day.

Sadly, perhaps induced by the offer of a large cash payment, he willingly lent his name to newspaper articles suggesting he'd accepted bribes to throw games against relegation-threatened teams while with City. His team-mates of the time reacted with disbelief and dismay – how could he concoct such an idea, they wondered.

If Paul did indeed accept money to help opponents, it was a terrible slur and a black mark on what had been a magnificent career. Paul was seemingly finished with football and football was certainly finished with him. The popular theory was that he'd made the story up, reeled in a Sunday newspaper and took the money – he'd burned his bridges and felt he had nothing to lose so why not make a few quid as well? Of course, if that was the case it was a terribly selfish act and an insult to his team-mates and the supporters of Manchester City who had idolised him.

He would earn his living from there on in driving miners to various pits, his heavy drinking never too far away. In 1974, in an interview with the *Manchester Evening News*, he told reporter Paul Hince: "I belong here in the Rhondda. Even when I was on top of the footballing world I always intended to come back here to live...yes, and to die!"

Roy Paul suffered with Alzheimer's disease in his later years, the last of which were spent in a nursing home in Glamorgan. He died in May, 2002 aged 80. The last words, fittingly, are those of his lifelong friend Roy Clarke.

"I doubt if City ever made a better signing," he said. "He was certainly regarded as the finest captain the club has ever had and nobody of my generation would argue with that.

"We used to call him 'Killer' and no player has ever acquired a more suitable nickname – and it wasn't just the opposition he frightened. Woe betide any City player who didn't pull his weight while Roy was skipper. If he thought you were letting the team down, you risked getting a back-hander!

"He was incredibly protective of his team-mates and if any City player was having trouble with an opponent, he'd switch positions for a few minutes and sort them out. He was a true leader of men and deserves to remebered as Manchester City's finest captain of all time."

Mike Doyle

1962-1978: 559 games, 40 goals

THE PHONE RANG and a journalist at a national newspaper sighed, put down his mug of tea and went over to answer it. "Hello?"

"If Mike Doyle plays at Old Trafford this weekend, he'll be shot and killed."

"Who is this?"

The caller hung up. The paper informed the police and the threat was taken seriously. Doyle was placed under 24-hour police protection in the days leading up to the game and he was advised it might be better not to play. Not a chance. Doyle played, City won – as usual – and the incident was largely forgotten. That was until the police, who'd be watching a known criminal for a number of weeks caught sight of him making a phone call in a public box. They made their move but he managed to run away, but was chased and caught by one of the officers. His colleague picked up the dangling phone and the person on the other end said the caller had just renewed his threat to kill Mike Doyle. A suspect was arrested and in his possession they found a handgun.

Urban legend or true? You decide.

BEING THE SON of a policeman in a tough neighbourhood was always going to attract problems and that's exactly the way it turned out for Mike Doyle. Pushed around and picked on, he could stand up for himself, but not against groups of four or five. Mike's dad, Tommy decided to give his son a little advantage and enrolled him in the police's self-defence classes where he learned the art of unarmed combat and gained a confidence that would serve him throughout his football career. Doyle already had attitude, now he had the right abilities to back it up – it made for an explosive combination that would take him all the way to the top in football.

Doyle's story began in earnest when he wrote to the *Manchester Evening News* after the paper had invited local youngsters to write in and say what they wanted to be when they grew up. Mike wrote in saying that he wanted to be a footballer or a PE teacher and unbeknown to him, Manchester City's chief scout, Harry Godwin, cut the letter out and put it among his clippings and letters from young hopefuls. It's a well-known story that a few years later while watching Stockport Boys, he enquired who the young half-back was and was told it was Michael Doyle. Godwin knew the name, but wasn't sure why. He went back to his office and sifted through his clippings until he found the letter bearing the lad's name and address so a few days later, he went around to his house. As he approached the front door he saw both a policeman's helmet and a Manchester City programme on a table near the window. He smiled to himself and knocked on the door, confident that the offer of a trial would be accepted – it was, and the skinny teenager signed on as an apprentice at Maine Road, beginning an 16-year association with the club he loved.

Doyle would become a a huge favourite among the City fans because of his attitude, style of play and outspoken comments. It's often been said that Doyle's blood ran blue and he was the embodiment of the fan on the terrace who had been given the chance to play for the club he supported and Doyle never forgot that. He didn't see himself as any different from the man on the street and he also spoke like the man on the street. His comments about Manchester United were legendary and they further enhanced his reputation as a cult hero.

He traced his dislike of United back to school, where he faced taunts due to City's lack of success during the late fifties and early sixties. He wanted to ram those words back down their throats and if he found an extra yard or managed one more lung-bursting surge from the back more than he normally did, it was because he was running on pure adrenaline.

On another occasion, during a youth cup semi-final against United, Doyle cleared the ball of the line only to see it rebound off Alf Wood's knee and into the net. George Best later claimed Doyle had "cried like a baby". He hadn't of course, but he saw it as a very public haranguing from Best and Doyle decided from there on that if that's how Best wanted to play it, it was open season.

He wasn't everyone's cup of tea and would have problems with rival fans, players, referees and even his own team-mates. An early taster of what lay ahead was when the young apprentice first met some of the senior sqaud in the dressing rooms at Maine Road prior to training. The Blues had made a disastrous start to the 1962/63 season, going down 8-1 at Wolverhampton Wanderers – and that with the great Bert Trautmann, who was coming towards the end of a magnificent career.

As the genial giant began to get changed, Doyle, who was sweeping the floor couldn't resist asking how Bert's back was after picking all those balls out of the net. Trautmann picked up Doyle and pinned him to the wall. "You keep your fucking mouth shut and just clean the boots."

A suitably chastised Doyle was then forced to wash Bert's bright yellow Volkswagen Beetle each week until the end of the season, but when the pair started playing reserve football together, following an impressive display by Doyle, the big German walked over and said "You'll be all right. You played well today. Keep it up."

There were other incidents in training, one where coach Jimmy Meadows almost cut the young Doyle in half with a tackle during five-a-side which ended with Meadows hanging Doyle on a coat-peg!

Doyle made his debut at Cardiff in 1965 and found himself in direct opposition to Welsh man-mountain John Charles and it wasn't long before he was on the end of a crunching challenge from the same man. He quickly learned how things are dealt with on the pitch when moments later his team-mate Johnny Crossan went over the top on Charles leaving him nursing a nasty set of stud marks down his thigh. "Take that you big Welsh nelly," whispered Crossan. If he didn't exactly court trouble, Mike Doyle never seemed too far away from it.

Joe Mercer and Malcolm Allison arrived the following season and they soon figured out who was worth keeping, who they could work on and who needed shipping out.

Allison could see Doyle had talent. He could tackle, win headers, had vision, pace and an eye for a goal. In fact, during the new management's first season in charge, a striker crisis saw Doyle put up front as an emergency striker – he scored six goals in four games! His 19 appearances helped the Blues to the Second Division championship and by 1968, Doyle was a first-team regular and a huge crowd favourite.

Of course, there was a whole team of crowd favourites and legends around then and 'The Holy Trinity' of Colin Bell, Francis Lee and Mike Summerbee were god-like figures to the City fans. Neil Young, Glyn Pardoe, Tony Book and Alan Oakes were also huge favourites, but of that team, Doyle was probably the outstanding Cult Hero. Bell, Lee and Summerbee are untouchable and Cult Hero status doesn't quite do them justice. They are club legends and there can be only a handful of players whose popularity is unquestioned. To be a Cult Hero, this writer believes, you have to have flaws either on or off the pitch.

If the fans have to be won over, so much the better. If the majority of supporters adore you, but there are pockets who have their doubts, again, the essence of the cult hero is further enhanced. Besides, what could be written about Colin, Buzzer and Franny that hasn't already been written These guys are the Untouchables – end of story.

Perhaps Tony Coleman might have given Doyle a good run for his money for the right to be the cult hero of the 67/68 championship side. Coleman's stay with City was brief, but never dull and Malcolm Allison labelled him as the "the nightmare of a delirious parole officer" and had once thrown a bed out of a window at Lilleshall. He'd punched a referee during a non-league match and been banned *sin die*, though he was later allowed to continue his career with Doncaster Rovers, the club City signed him from.

Coleman joined City towards the end of the 1966/67 season and Maine Road was the closest thing he ever had to a spiritual home. With his blond Beatles haircut, the scoundrel scouser went from one scrape to another. He once turned up to the ground in a bright yellow Ford Zodiac, much to the dismay of manager Joe Mercer.

"Bloody hell, son, why did you get a car in that colour?" he asked. "For god's sake get it toned down." The following day, Coleman turned up with the car now a two-tone bright yellow and purple. Mercer just shook his head and walked away.

If 'TC' – as he was better known – had been a Manchester lad, he might well have given Doyle a good run for his money for the title of cult hero from this period. But, like Johnny Crossan before him, he didn't stay more than a few seasons and though both men were hugely popular, a dyed-in-the-wool Blue was always going to edge it.

Doyle's longevity and his passionate hatred for all things Manchester United made him the fans' hero for different reasons. He would taunt the United players and supporters prior to derby games, winding them up to the point he'd received sackfuls of hate mail from disgruntled Reds, which, of course, only further increased his currency with City fans. The thing was, most of what he claimed was true – George Best wasn't a threat to City because Tony Book usually marked him out of the game and the Blues regularly won at Old Trafford during that period.

Press coverage, even back in the sixties, was heavily biased in favour of United and that irked the City players, but none more so than Doyle. Returning from a European Cup Winners' Cup tie against SK Lierse, the players began to read the early editions of the English papers, fully expecting their 3-0 win over the Belgians to be the headline news, especially as the Blues were the only English side still in Europe. But to a man, they read the papers with something approaching snarls on their faces as the headlines in several papers were all about Manchester United's fightback... in a testimonial! City were afforded a small column in an inside page but it was moments like that that galvanised the team – but Doyle in particular who would continue to stew for weeks. First to bear the brunt, however, were the drunken hacks who'd travelled with the team to Belgium. Mike Summerbee and Doyle gave them a verbal lashing about the pathetic coverage and one of the reporters suggested he should say what he really felt. "I'll tell you how I feel," said Doyle. "I fucking hate them! Simple as that." Doyle thought no more about it until the next day when he saw the headlines 'Doyle Hates United'. He was surprised initially, then just thought 'what the hell'. In for a penny, as they say. He would vent his anger in the form of continued rants in the press about how inept and unimportant United were.

He had his windows smashed, tyres slashed and, as mentioned earlier, received death threats but was still unrepentant. Basically, he didn't care. A hard-drinking womaniser would not be an inaccurate description of Doyle during his City career, but he never gave less than his all and would happily have died representing his club on the pitch. He once said: "I'm the man off the terraces who has been given the chance of playing for the club I love." He was, in effect, living the dream.

The City fans lapped it up. Not only was their team top dogs, but their idol was rubbing their noses in the mud at every opportunity. After a 4-1 win at Old Trafford in December 1970, Doyle told reporters: "That was easier than I expected." Doyle had scored one of the goals that day and had run in front of the Stretford End with his arms raised, receiving a volley of abuse for his troubles and 20,000 V-signs from disgruntled Reds. Doyle had claimed there was only one team of any importance in Manchester these days and , prior to the game, responding to questions of why he celebrated in such a manner, said: "They'd been jibing me all week after I aired my views so I just thought I'd give them a taste of their own medicine and remind them that everything I'd said was true." During that same game, only the intervention of Tony Book and Brian Kidd stopped Doyle throttling George Best, who had just committed an horrendous challenge on his best mate Glyn Pardoe.

The tackle would, in effect, be the beginning of the end for Pardoe who never quite regained full fitness and, but for the expertise of a surgeon, might well have lost a leg. Doyle saw red that day and freely admitted that he intended to kill Best – en exaggeration, of course, but he may well have put the United legend in the bed alongside Pardoe had he not been held back.

He was once red carded in a Manchester derby following a bout of handbags with Lou Macari. It was an icy surface and Doyle lost his footing and slid into Macari who toppled over. Macari pushed the ball into Doyle's chest and the City man placed the ball on the floor and retreated towards his area for the free kick. Referee Clive 'The Book' Thomas called both players over, they smiled at each other expecting a telling off , but they were wrong. "You threw a punch at Doyle and he responded and threw a punch back. I'm sending you both off." Both Doyle and Macari pleaded their innocence and then both walked away saying they weren't going off. Thomas ordered the two captains, Martin Buchan and Doyle to approach him whereby he duly ordered both teams off the pitch. It was a bizarre situation but when City boss Ron Saunders asked if both teams would be resuming with 11 players, Thomas said that the two players he'd sent off stayed off.

Doyle's blunt comments didn't always just irk the opposition, either. It was a long time before Joe Corrigan forgave him for asking the bench why he was being picked during a particularly stormy game at Burnley in 1973. Corrigan allowed a gentle back pass to slip through his fingers and roll over the line. Doyle ran to the bench and it must have had some bearing on manager Johnny Hart's thinking because just over a fortnight later, City paid £100,000 for Motherwell's Keith MacRae – equalling the British transfer record for a goalkeeper. The outburst could have meant the end for Corrigan and it would be a long time before he forgave Doyle, though his comments that he thought Joe had gone from the worst keeper he'd ever seen, to one of the best, calmed down the situation somewhat.

Doyle was once sent off for punching Leighton James as City took on Derby County. The irony was, it was one of the rare occasions he didn't actually do anything! He tackled James with venom and as James got up, Doyle reckoned he was about to spit at him. "Don't even think about it," Doyle told him and pushed him away. With that, James collapsed to the ground – Robbie Savage would have been proud – shouting: "He cuffed me! He cuffed me!" – which ensured a red card for Doyle who left the pitch infuriated – but the story doesn't end there. By way of coincidence, not long after the incident, Leighton James and his Derby team-mates happened to be staying in Blackpool as well as part of a winding-down excercise. As Doyle and Mike Summerbee walked into the foyer of the Savoy nightclub, who should walk out of the toilets but Leighton James? The pair made eye contact and the story goes that James, white as a sheet, sprinted for safety by running through the nightclub and out of the fire exit before Doyle could begin his pursuit in earnest.

Another player Doyle never saw eye-to-eye with was Rodney Marsh. Doyle didn't appreciate Marsh's flash attitude, clothes and car and felt he looked down on his hometown and the people who inhabited it. That may or may not have been true, but there could be no doubting that Manchester was a million miles behind London back in those days and it must have been something of a culture shock for Marsh.

Perhaps Marsh being given the captaincy over Doyle for the 1974/75 season also didn't sit too well. Here was a player whose blood ran blue being overlooked for a flash Cockney who was just out for himself – that's how Doyle, who also thought Marsh was the reason City missed out on another league title in 1972, saw it.

When Marsh was relieved of the captaincy in 1975, Doyle was handed the armband and wasted no time in talking to the press and let Marsh have both barrels. Th enext day the headlines read 'Doyle Slates Lazy Marsh' – but Doyle wasn't concerned about that. He just wanted what was best for Manchester City and who could fault him for that?

He had run-ins with journalists, flooring one drunken hack on a tour of Australia after he'd overstepped the mark with some of his comments about the City players treating the tour as one big booze-up. Mike Summerbee had a go at him and the reporter, an Irishman exiled Down Under, then failed to toast the Queen – not a good idea when a patriot like Mike Doyle is around. Doyle had had enough and went to the toilet. The reporter followed him and told him that if Summerbee didn't take back his comment that he worked for a comic, he publish a story that te whole team were drunks. With that, the reporter threw a punch which Doyle ducked and then and cracked him one on the jaw, sending him down several steps into the toilet.

Another time, he was having a quiet meal with some friends when three men and a woman began taunting him about an injury he'd picked up at West Ham. One in particular became a bit mouthy and Doyle warned him to let it go – he didn't and shouted over to Doyle 'I hope you've broken your leg.' City's famous No.4 limped over to the bloke and punched him. Well, he had been warned... Doyle didn't take any shit off anybody.

Doyle was an inspirational captain – he'd been born to lead City and during his first season as skipper, he led the team to a 2-1 success in the 1976 League Cup final against Newcastle United. There was no prouder man in Manchester and he enjoyed the moment to the full, celebrating with the fans on and off the pitch. Internationally, he had been put on stand by for the 1970 World Cup in Mexico, but his wife was seriously ill and he remained in England, believing his chance would come again. It did, but not until 1976 when he won the first of five caps for his country – a pitiful return for such a hard-working and talented defender.

The following season, he and defensive partner Dave Watson forged one of the best centre-back pairings the club has ever had and together they helped City to within a point of eventual champions Liverpool – it was a fantastic achievement. He was rushed back from injury too soon towards the end of the 1976/77 campaign and it would cost him dearly the following year and, eventually signalled the end of his career at City. He struggled to regain fitness during 77/78 and the man who once threatened to quit City if he was sold (shortly after Marsh's arrival), finally severed his ties with the club and joined Stoke for just £50,000.

He played in every major final between 1969 and 1976 – five in total, to add to his championship medal and scored one of City's goals in 1970 League Cup victory over West Brom. He played part of the European Cup Winners' Cup final before badly damaging his ankle tendon before being carried off agony. During City's golden era, he was always there, fighting for the cause, stirring it up and giving 100 per cent. There have been few players dedicated to one club in quite the way Doyle was to Manchester City and his is an extinct breed in the modern game. He ate, slept and breathed Manchester City and the fans adored him for it. He was, after all, their very own representative out on the pitch.

Joe Corrigan

1966-1983: 592 games, 0 goals

"SOD OFF CORRIGAN, you're bloody useless!" came the shout, almost down his ear hole, from dozens of fans on the terraces. "You're not fit to lace his boots!" yelled somebody else. Joe was becoming used to the abuse and determined to ride the taunts about his ability and the cruel jibes about his weight. It was part and parcel of football, but this particular evening, the insults had come from Manchester City fans. It was during Johnny Hart's testimonial in 1973 and Maine Road was filled with perhaps 20,000 fans who'd come to pay their respects to the former player, coach and manager who'd been forced to retire due to ill-health.

The idea had been to let arguably the greatest goalkeeper of all-time, Bert Trautmann, play one half and then Joe play the second. However, as Corrigan walked around the cinder track to see whether Bert, who had been in retirement for several years, was ready to come off yet, he was subjected to the kind of heckling usually reserved for players from opposing teams. He was almost at the end of his tether and was considering earning his living either elsewhere or doing something else entirely. Later, as the players enjoyed an after-match drink, Trautmann found the young keeper and said "don't worry about what people say – people forget that I started by making mistakes and it took time for me to find my feet. In years to come, nobody will be thinking of the mistakes you made." Joe decided that if a legend like Bert Trautmann reckoned he'd one day win the fans over, he would make sure he did everything he could to win their respect and began a mission that would result in him being one of the best goalkeepers in the world.

SOME PLAYERS FIT better into the category of Cult Heroes better than others, while some are considered club legends. Colin Bell, Mike Summerbee and Francis Lee are legends, mostly because they played such crucial roles during City's most successful era from 1967 to 1970. Few can justifiably be described as both, but one player in particular fits quite snugly – Joe Corrigan.

The giant goalkeeper endured and enjoyed the full spectrum of emotions with the City fans over an epic 17-year stay at Maine Road where he went quite literally from zero to hero. Everybody will have their own definition of heroes and legends and for many, there won't be much between either category. But if there is a difference, it could be that many of the Cult Heroes in this book have attained their status because they've had to battle hard to change opinions, win over the fans and the cult of their popularity is something of a slow-burner that matures like a fine wine.

Corrigan signed for City after being spotted playing for Sale FC. A tall, stocky lad, he was forced to play rugby union throughout his schooldays and the only football he was able to play was either during break time or on the croft outside his home where he'd volunteer to play in goal in knockabouts with a group of mates.

He enjoyed throwing himself around on the muddy patch of ground and he was deemed good enough to sign for amateur side Sale, though his size dictated he should play as centre-half, initially. He scored three goals on his debut for Sale and his father bought him a new pair of boots on the strength of that performance. He did well for Sale – it was a decent standard and the teenager was holding his own against men much older than he was. Then one occasion, when the regular keeper – a little fellow called Ernie – failed to turn up, Joe went in goal and remained between the sticks for the team from then on. Fate had dealt him his first hand.

He was being groomed as an apprentice for a life at a huge Manchester electronics firm and would play as a centre-half during inter-departmental games at Trafford Park and would fool around in goals during the half-time break. It was, amazingly, on the strength of one such brief mess-around in goal that he was offered a trial with Manchester City after which he was offered a contract – a shock to the system to Joe's family and friends who were almost exclusively Manchester United fans. A work colleague who'd played for the Army national team, saw the youngster's potential and as he also did a bit of scouting for the local league sides, he asked Joe if he'd like a trial with Manchester City. Joe didn't take the offer seriously and all but dismissed the offer, but his colleague was a as good as his word and set up the trial. In fact, a week after he'd agreed to join City, a card dropped through his front door offering him a trial at Old Trafford but there was never a chance he'd take up the offer.

City's legendary chief scout Harry Godwin told Joe Mercer that Joe would either turn out to be "a joke or a cracker," but he had a gut feeling that the 6ft 4in giant from Sale would be the latter rather than the former.

He was promising without being outstanding and he was signed as a youth goalkeeper with the likes of Harry Dowd, Ken Mulhearn and Alan Ogley all ahead of him in the pecking order. Within a year, however, a crisis meant that he was given his senior debut in a League Cup tie at home to Blackpool in October 1967 and it was during that match that perhaps the shaky foundations to his early years at City were laid. Joe allowed a fairly tame shot to squeeze through his hands, through his legs and over the line for a Blackpool goal – it was virtually his first touch!

The supporters who were present that night had hardly had time to form an opinion on the young custodian before he was picking the ball out of the back of the net following an embarrassing error. It wasn't fair to pass judgement on a player fresh out of the youth team making his first-team debut, but nonetheless, the seeds of doubt had been sewn and, as they say, first impressions tend to last.

Corrigan also had the added millstone of Bert Trautmann and Frank Swift around his neck. There were still a large number of supporters who remembered both players and had watched them in action and any new boy would be sized up against two such legendary figures. Trautmann and Swift were icons and they cast a sizeable shadow over any new recruits, many of whom were unfairly weighed up against but even more so when coach Malcolm Allison claimed Joe would be better than both men!

Joe never made a league appearance for the Blues during their championship season, with the popular Dowd and Mulhearn sharing first-team duties and instead went out on loan to Shrewsbury Town for a while. At Gay Meadow, he was soon under the tutelage of manager Harry Gregg, the legendary former Manchester United goalkeeper. Gregg passed on all his knowledge to the youngster who saw an immediate improvement in his game. He also helped Joe slim down by a stone, again improving his game.

He returned to Maine Road unsure of his future, but at least knowing that Malcolm Allison reckoned he had the makings of a top class goalie. He made his senior league debut the following campaign, in a 2-1 defeat at Ipswich and also played in the 1-0 defeats at Nottingham Forest and Leeds United before finally keeping a clean sheet in his fourth appearance of the season – the last game of 1968/69, in a 1-0 win over Liverpool. City's league form had been unimpressive as defending champions and they'd finished a disappointing thirteenth, though the young goalkeeper had made quite an impression when he kept goal against Leeds' Jack Charlton who said he couldn't recall being beaten so easily in the air before. "It was quite frustrating for me," said the England legend. "The boy just picked them off my forehead. Normally I can put the goalkeeper off but I didn't worry him."

As Dowd and Mulhearn's careers with the Blues began to tail off dramatically, so Corrigan's began in earnest and despite very little experience of league football, Malcolm Allison threw him in at the deep end for the 69/70 campaign. Allison's belief was total and he would tell the media that he had "manufactured" Joe into being a goalkeeper.

It was a memorable first full season and though Corrigan had not made a bond with the fans as yet, he kept goal in 34 out of 42 league game and was selected by Sir Alf Ramsey for an England Under-23 clash with Russia at Old Trafford. City won the FA Cup that season, but Mercer and Allison had played Harry Dowd in every round so it was only fair he kept his place in the 1-0 win over Leicester City.

But there had been one very public gaffe by the young custodian towards the end of the 1969/70 season and it would be one that would be replayed over and over with the *Match of the Day* cameras in town for the attractive looking City v West Ham United clash in March 1970. Corrigan punted the ball down field and turned back to walk to his goals. As he did the ball flew over his shoulder and into the net – the Hammers' Ronnie Boyce had volleyed the ball straight back and scored a spectacular goal as West Ham romped home 5-1.

It was nothing short of disastrous and the dissenters began to shuffle uneasily at the prospect of Corrigan in goal for the foreseeable future. The fans forgave, if not forget, however, as City won both the League Cup and European Cup Winners' Cup that season with the 21-year-old Corrigan collecting two winners' medals in the space of just a few weeks. It had been an incredible season for Corrigan.

But those two cup successes would be the last for a while as the successful side of the late sixties began to fragment and age. The patchy form in the league meant that the fans were reluctant to turn on the players who'd brought them a cabinet full of trophies and the more established stars in the side had earned a sizeable credit balance with the supporters that could carry them through the lean, trophy-less years. Players like Colin Bell, Franny Lee and Mike Summerbee were pretty much untouchable anyway whereas Corrigan had, in many ways, started in debt and was struggling to get in the black.

There was no doubt that some fans still viewed him with suspicion - and his frame also seemed to be filling out at an alarming rate. He was a sitting duck and as the supporters found it difficult to return to league also-rans as the glory years came to an abrupt halt, so some of them felt they needed to vent their frustration on one or two of the upcoming youngsters. Ian Bowyer and Joe Corrigan were entering choppy waters and every mistake seemed to be magnified a thousand times and in Bowyer's case, the only choice he was left with was to find another club, which he duly did, joining Orient after an unhappy few seasons.

With Bowyer gone, Corrigan was now on his own and bearing the full brunt of the crowd's frustration. Despite his size, he wasn't the type to vent his frustrations in the press and instead drew further within himself as he sought to ride out the storm.

Malcolm Allison kept believing in Corrigan and refused to bring in a fresh face, but when Big Mal quit the Blues in 1973, new manager Johnny Hart felt Corrigan needed competition and after a poor display in a 3-0 defeat to Burnley, the Blues stumped up £100,000 for Motherwell's Keith MacRae. It was a joint record fee (equal with Leeds' Gary Sprake) for a goalkeeper.

MacRae took over in goal for the majority of the 1973/74 campaign and also played at Wembley as City went down 2-1 to Wolves in the League Cup final that season, under yet another new manager – the strict disciplinarian Ron Saunders, who lasted a matter of months before being forced out by player power. He was replaced by Tony Book who promised to give Corrigan another crack at being the undisputed No.1 and he played him in the last two games of 73/74, the last of which was the famous 1-0 win over Manchester United that confirmed the Reds' relegation.

MacRae's arrival galvanised Corrigan and made him more determined than ever to win back his place and the City supporters' respect. He trained harder, lost weight (a broken jaw in training helped speed up his new slimline look as he was forced to eat his meals through a straw) and by the time he was recalled for the remainder of the 1974/75 campaign, he looked a completely different player.

The team was beginning to pick up, too, under the management of Book, who initially turned to MacRae – possibly due to boardroom pressure – they didn't want a record for the first half of the 1975/76 season until injury gave Joe another chance to stake his claim. He played well but after half-a-dozen games, he was dropped and MacRae reinstated – and this after a 5-1 win over Newcastle United. MacRae let four goals in on his return and 24 hours later Joe announced that he was quitting City and demanded a transfer.

He was fined two weeks' wages for his outburst in the media and transfer listed by Book. Corrigan didn't care – he wanted out and if he didn't get his way, he'd quit the game completely. He felt there were factions at the club who didn't want him to play and his failure to win over a section of the supporters had finally worn him down.

But an injury to MacRae meant another recall for the want-away keeper and he showed guts, courage and professionalism by the bucketload to return and play superbly well – so much so he would never be dropped again from the first team and missed just one league game over the next five years. It was an astonishing comeback and it won the giant custodian a huge amount of respect among the supporters.

To complete an incredible turnaround, Corrigan was voted Player of the Year by the City fans for his displays during the 1975/76 campaign. The following season he picked up his second winner's medal as City won the '76 League Cup with a 2-1 win over Newcastle United. He also won his first full England cap, coming on as a second half substitute against Italy in New York. His form and bravery had turned virtually all the doubters into believers and by season 1976/77 the dramatic transformation in Joe Corrigan was complete as he had by then become the rock of Book's talented side. City missed out on the league title by a single point to Liverpool and Corrigan was, by this time, considered to be one of the top three keepers in the country and an England squad regular.

Corrigan's consistency and brilliance was largely down to a change in attitude and his weight loss. His agility improved dramatically and the occasional lapse in concentration, not dissimilar to the problems David James would have throughout his career, were eliminated from his game. The hate mail had turned to fan mail and he became City's Mr Dependable with his bravery winning him an army of new admirers.

What poor Keith MacRae must have made of the situation isn't hard to fathom – why hadn't he become the hero? Hadn't he arrived as one of the most expensive keepers in the world? Who can say why one player excels and another sees his career fade away into nothing, but that's exactly what happened to MacRae, a steady enough goalie who did his job quietly and well enough. But he wasn't Joe Corrigan and the truth is, he wasn't in his league and when the supporters realised as much, they threw their collective weight behind the lad who'd progressed from the youth team and was, in effect, one of their own.

If there's one thing City fans love, it's triumph over adversity. It was plain as day to see that Corrigan had worked hard to become this good and he'd never once publicly complained about the often harsh treatment he'd received from his own fans. Internationally, he was desperately unlucky to have two top keepers ahead of him in the race to keep goal for England in the shape of Ray Clemence and Peter Shilton. The pair, who both were behind fantastic defences at Liverpool and Nottingham Forest respectively, were monopolising the England No.1 spot and national boss Ron Greenwood found it difficult to see past the two talented custodians. Subsequently, Corrigan was left with the odd scrap here and there, earning a paltry nine caps plus another 10 England 'B' appearances when he would have earned 50-plus had he represented any other country at the time. The fact that his first full appearance for England came in 1978 against Brazil is scandalous.

The international disappointment only seemed to enhance Corrigan's reputation among the Blues' faithful who shouted 'England's, England's No.1!' every time he played. He also was very much a man of the people and was down to earth and approachable. Manchester City without Joe Corrigan in goals was unthinkable during the seventies and he won his second Player of the Year award in 1978.

He struck up a warm friendship with 'Big Helen' – Helen Turner, a well-known City fanatic who rang a bell during matches whenever she felt the lads needed a lift.

Helen, a market flower seller, would present Joe with a lucky sprig of heather before each home game and it would become an endearing part of the Maine Road folklore over a period of years.

Joe also had the habit of crouching down on his haunches and facing his own goal whenever City were awarded a penalty, jumping up and punching the air if he saw or heard the Blues' supporters celebrating after the spot-kick had been struck.

The millstone of Trautmann and Swift had been a heavy one, but Corrigan had done the impossible by carrying it on his broad shoulders for almost a decade and then joining their elite club of goalkeeping greats. Without question, he was one of the main reasons the Blues were such a force during the seventies. He was also a gentle giant, quiet and unassuming enough to become the president of the Junior Blues, a role he took very seriously and gave up a large proportion of his spare time to be involved with various events and fundraisers for the awe-struck youngsters.

His consistency throughout that decade earned him respect throughout the game and was often afforded a warm welcome by opposing fans on away grounds, a source of great pride to his own supporters and he at least enjoyed a sustained spell during that time when he was part of one of the best teams in the country.

Yet despite the team being packed with crowd favourites, it was Joe Corrigan that the fans idolised above all others – quite a feat when you consider Dennis Tueart, Peter Barnes, Asa Hartford and Dave Watson were among his team-mates.

It's telling, too, that when Malcolm Allison returned to Maine Road in 1979 and proceeded to dismantle a hugely talented side packed with established internationals, virtually the only survivor of the big-name cull was Joe Corrigan. Allison hadn't forgotten how the big man had shown guts and stood up against everything that was thrown at him and he wasn't about to cast aside such a formidable asset – he may have axed more than half a dozen top stars, but perhaps he felt with Big Joe keeping goal, he'd be on safe ground with his somewhat bizarre transfer policy.

As it turned out, Allison's stay was a disaster and after Corrigan publicly slated Allison's transfer policy and suggested his return was a grave error of judgement - the club initially suspended him, then fined him two weeks' wages. He was too important to leave out, though and he remained the first-choice keeper and the Blues just escaped relegation in 1979/80 and were well on their way to Division Two before Allison was sacked and John Bond took the helm.

Bond, too, kept the big man as his No.1 and it was Corrigan that kept goal in the Centenary FA Cup final in 1981 and subsequent replay – some 13 years after he first played his first game for the Blues and a further indication of his longevity as a top-level performer. Corrigan was magnificent in both games against Tottenham and didn't deserve to be on the losing side.

Even with the talented youngster Alex Williams knocking on the first team door, Corrigan began his seventeenth year at Maine Road as the first choice goalkeeper, but by this point was getting itchy feet. The team was in terminal decline and though he wanted to broaden his horizons before it was too late, he still wanted to stay and see out the 1982/83 campaign and ensure the Blues retained their top-flight status. After 17 years at Maine Road he wasn't about to turn his back on the club he clearly loved. Incredibly, the Blues elected to allow Corrigan to join Seattle Sounders in the North American Soccer League in March 1983, despite his offer to remain until the final match of the campaign had been played. The rookie Williams was pitched in and though it's no reflection on his considerable ability, he found it hard to prevent the inevitable and two months after Big Joe's departure, City were relegated.

Many put it down to Corrigan's absence and they may well have been correct. He wasn't just a fantastic goalkeeper, his presence was all encompassing and his influence on the back four was immense. Things didn't go that well for Joe in the States as Seattle headed towards bankruptcy. It was a cruel blow for Joe who deserved better and had enjoyed his brief stay in the States. He returned to England with Brighton and Hove Albion in time for the 1983/84 season. Just three months later he was back at Maine Road to face City and the standing ovation he received from the supporters lasted several minutes.

It was the first time they'd had the chance to thank the Big Man who had once made 197 consecutive senior league appearances plus given almost two decades of sterling service. Though the Blues ran out 4-0 winners that day, it was the returning hero that occupied the thoughts of most of the supporters as they made their way home through the dark, rainy Moss Side streets. He later went on to become a top goalkeeper coach at clubs such as Celtic, Liverpool and West Brom. Sadly, the call from City never came and they turned instead to Alex Stepney – an odd choice to say the least.

Rodney Marsh

1972-1975: 144 games, 46 goals

SOCKS ROLLED DOWN his ankles, trudging towards the dressing rooms, Rodney Marsh cut a lonely figure when he decided to snub the presentation ceremony at the end of the 1974 League Cup final. Marsh had done his best, but City had lost 2-1 to Wolverhampton Wanderers and the disappointment hit him hard. While the other City players stayed to applaud Wolves as they collected the trophy, Marsh was even booed by his own supporters for this unsporting behaviour. But Marsh was, and always has been a law unto himself. Was he trying to attract attention to himself, even in the midst of a morale-crushing defeat? Only Rodney could answer that. He foraged a lonely path for most of his career –the word individualistic could have been invented specifically for him. Adored, despised, respected and selfish – he's heard it all, but one thing that could never be denied is that Rodney Marsh was an entertainer and football is a spectator sport, after all. He put bums on seats and the fans lapped it up. Capable of genius and incredibly lacklustre displays, there wasn't much middle ground with the man whose name echoed around the Kippax long after he'd gone. Like him or loathe him, the man was a football genius...

"I NEVER WANTED to sign Rodney, you know Tommy. It was all Malcolm's doing." Joe Mercer squinted into the Hoylake sunshine and struck his ball towards the tiny patch of lush green turf in the distance. The Tommy in question was Mike Doyle and Genial Joe had a captive audience. Doyle had never liked Marsh – he thought he could play, but there was something about him he could never take to. Too flash for his liking. The men played their game but the revelation had come as no surprise to Doyle. Marsh has Big Mal stamped all over him and the pair were two of a kind, some might label them Champagne Charlies but nobody doubted their ability. They were two of a kind and when things were rough at Maine Road and Big Mal, by then manager of the Blues, was under severe pressure from the board, Marsh stated "If Malcolm goes, I'll quit, too."

Born 11 October 1944 in London's East End, Marsh was a docker's son from Stepney. He lived and breathed football from an early age and always wanted to be the star man in the team. He practised tricks and was blessed with a natural ability that made him stand out a mile in junior matches. A bright lad, he turned down the chance to go to grammar school because they only played rugby, which he hated. He knew his path to stardom was assured and he wouldn't do anything that might end his dream of becoming a professional footballer. He began his career aged 17, when he signed for Fulham and made his debut against Aston Villa in 1963 and he made an immediate impression. "We won 1-0 and I scored the only goal," he recalled. "Was it a good goal? No, it was a brilliant goal – a right-foot volley 25 yards out into the top corner on 61 minutes."

Rodney not only played a good game, he talked a good game, too. Always has. He learned his trade at Craven Cottage under the watchful eye of the great Johnny Haynes, Marsh's idol, and the raw youngster studied Haynes' technique and learned all he could from him. "His standards were incredibly high," he said of Haynes, "both in what he asked of himself and of others."

In 1966, aged 21, Marsh transferred to QPR and it was while at Loftus Road that his star really began to shine. Rangers may have been in the Third Division, but Marsh's signing seemed to be the icing on the cake for a side that would cause one of the biggest cup upsets of all time.

"There was a time, between 1967 and 1969, when QPR were unbeatable," said Marsh. "We won promotion in successive seasons and also reached the League Cup final in '67 where we played West Bromwich Albion."

A spectacular goal at Wembley often does wonders for one's career and if anyone was likely to seize the moment, it was Marsh. Though West Brom led 2-0 at the break, Rangers fought back and it was Marsh who levelled the scores with a goal that remains as crystal clear in his mind today as it were yesterday. "I picked up a long pass out of defence about 40 yards from their goal," he recalled. "I turned my marker, went to the left, went to the right, beat a couple of other players along the way and then suddenly, from 25 yards, hit a shot that skimmed across the Wembley surface, hit the inside of the post and went in. It was pandemonium."

He continued to enthral, frustrate and delight in equal measures before winning his first England cap against Switzerland in 1972. Shortly after he became only the fourth player to transfer for a fee of £200,000 or more when Malcolm Allison brought the mercurial forward to Maine Road, just 24 hours before the transfer deadline, for what seemed likely to be the title run-in. It was March 1972 and the Blues were clear at the top of the table with just nine games to go. Six wins would land the title and Allison reckoned Marsh's arrival would be icing on the cake, but the move was to spectacularly backfire.

The deal was clinched in a 45-minute meeting at a London hotel and it was a club record for City. Allison, who had tracked the player for four years, was convinced Marsh could be City's answer to George Best and he thought he'd also add 10,000 to the gate at Maine Road. Joe Mercer wasn't convinced that Marsh would be good for the team and besides, why even take the risk of failure when things were going so well. But Joe trusted Malcolm's reasoning and he put up a great case for Marsh's signing.

"This has been a tremendously successful day for me," said Allison. "I'm delighted we came to a quick agreement with QPR. Rodney is a great character and a Cockney. That means there will be two Cockneys at Maine Road – him and me. We can keep each other company."

Those words, perhaps said more about the deal than anything else. It seemed as though Big Mal had just purchased an expensive toy for himself and he couldn't wait to use it. It was perhaps the most self-indulgent signing the club has ever made and it would come at a heavy price, far outweighing the fee paid.

Marsh would no longer be the big fish in the small pond, either. He was joining a club brimming with talent and in Colin Bell, Francis Lee and Mike Summerbee, three of the greatest talents of the era. Lee saw no harm at all in Marsh's arrival and said: "To bring the best out of his style of play, I think City is the only club he could go to. I think his signing is an exciting prospect."

Yet he was joining a squad of largely tough northerners with a tremendous work ethic. They played as a team and despite the talent at the club, there were no superstars and all got on well together. It was an ageing side, but they certainly had one last hurrah in them and a desire to prove the cynics wrong by landing the league championship for a second time in just four years. They topped the division through hard work, though there were plenty of match winners in the team. Young Tony Towers had broken into the side and was having a fantastic season – many felt City could only lose the title and in that respect, Allison was taking a spectacular gamble. The irony was, City had nearly signed Marsh before the start of the season for a fee of £154,000 – had he enjoyed a pre-season with his team-mates, learned how they played and the team understood better how he played and could fit into the side, things may have been very different. The offer, however, was considered too low and the deal was put on ice.

Allison couldn't wait to get Marsh into the side and despite not quite recovering from a slight groin strain and not being totally fit, he was plunged into the home game with Chelsea, with Towers relegated to the bench. More than 53,000 turned out to see his home debut – some 10,000 above the average attendance that season, and City edged the game 1-0. Yet it was clear from the word go that Marsh's arrival was interrupting the fast counter-attacking style of the team, with Marsh collecting the ball out wide and holding up the ball as he attempted to beat his marker.

During the next three games, City took just one point, drawing at Newcastle before disastrously losing at home to Stoke City and then at Southampton. The impetus had been lost and the Blues were off the top. Marsh showed his talent in the next game, scoring twice in a 3-1 home win over West Ham, but was on the bench at Old Trafford for the Manchester derby. Allison had told Marsh he would play at least half the game and Mike Doyle was the man to make way. City won 3-1 and Marsh scored again, though he was left out of the side that drew at Coventry he was back for the trip to Ipswich, where the title hopes completely disappeared in a 2-1 defeat. The Blues ended the campaign by beating champions Derby 2-0, but ended fourth in the final standings.

The finger was pointed squarely at one man – unfairly, of course – but it was Rodney Marsh who was blamed for losing the title in 1972. Marsh later admitted he was the reason behind the slump in form. "I changed the way Manchester City played football," he said. "When I joined them they were a well-oiled machine, well co-ordinated and well organised. But what they didn't have, and I hate to say this, was star quality and that was what I was supposed to provide and although I provided it, it was to the detriment of team play.

"They started to play around me and we lost the focus of what we were trying to do. I hold my hand up to say I was the responsible for City losing the championship in 1972."

The dye had been cast and his relationship with the club, supporters and team-mates would be filled with controversy from there on in. It would never be dull, though.

To Marsh, Manchester had something of a claustrophobic feel to it. Back then, there wasn't that much to do and wherever he went, he was under the spotlight. His clothes were different, his hair was different, his car was different and his outlook on life was different. Yet Rodney Marsh was perhaps the closest thing to a living embodiment of Manchester City Football Club.

He was mercurial, unpredictable and a lovable rogue. To not like Marsh was to not like football. He was, at times, magical to watch and pure entertainment. The fans fell in love with him and though at times it was a rocky affair, it was a match made in heaven. Fate had set a course for City and they weren't meant to win the league title that year, end of story. It wasn't the end of Rodney Marsh, however, whose colourful stay with the Blues had only just begun.

He admitted he felt like an outsider and was close to asking for a transfer just a few weeks into his City career but he got on with it and things began to improve during his first full season with the Blues. Joe Mercer had gone and Allison was now in sole charge so there was never any danger of him not being included, but seven defeats from the first three games of the 1972/73 season didn't bode well for the new manager. In fact, things went from bad to worse and there seemed a possibility at one point that City might even lose their top-flight status.

A year after joining, and with Allison teetering on the brink, he spoke out on a regional soccer show *Kick Off*, saying that if Malcolm went, he'd go to. It was understandable because up to that point, his time in Manchester had been largely disappointing. A fifth round FA Cup exit at Sunderland effectively ended the

Blues' season and on 22 March, Allison and City parted company, Two weeks later, Marsh slapped in a transfer request. "This had to happen," he said. "It's best for me and best for the club. It's no good when you don't feel free and happy in what you do. There were problems when Malcolm was here, but I felt I could cope, then. He gave me some extra strength because he'd shown such tremendous confidence in me and when he left, he took something with him as far as I was concerned."

Marsh didn't leave and finished the season as joint-top scorer with Franny Lee on 14 goals from 37 starts. New manager Johnny Hart lasted a matter of months into the 1973/74 campaign before Ron Saunders took the reins.

Marsh, by this time, had won over the majority of his team-mates (Mike Doyle not withstanding) and was starting to look like a £200,000 player at long last. Hart had given Marsh a more adventurous role within his side, ensuring he got the best out of him by keeping him in the thick of the action. The transfer request was torn up and both player and club moved on, but with Rodney Marsh, controversy was never far away.

His ball-juggling tricks on the wing coupled with some outrageous piss-taking had made Marsh the new darling of the Kippax. They sang his name to the tune of Chicory Tip's Son of my Father, chanting 'Oh, Rodney, Rodney. Rodney, Rodney, Rodney, Rodney, Rodney Marsh!' Marsh admitted the hairs on his neck stood on end every time he heard it.

As City progressed through the rounds in the League Cup, Marsh played with a cartilage problem and made it to play in the final against Wolves, where his efforts didn't find reward in a 2-1 defeat. His decision to walk to the changing rooms instead of congratulating the winners and collecting his loser's tankard once again caused a rift among certain senior players. Marsh later apologised for his actions. "I'm a bad loser and I just felt sick about the whole situation," his said in his own defence. "If I upset anybody, I apologise." The fact was Marsh had opened up one or two old wounds and it wouldn't be quite as easy to paper over the cracks this time. He played just once more that season before being ruled out with injury for the remaining games.

Saunders was sacked and replaced by Tony Book and the legendary former skipper thought long and hard about how he could make best use of Marsh and his decision shocked a lot of people – he made him captain. It was an inspirational and brave choice by the rookie manager, but he felt the added responsibility would help Marsh settle down and also make him a better team player.

Surprisingly, Marsh took to the role well and started in dazzling fashion, scoring two during a 4-0 opening day win over West Ham. The team responded well, too, and for a time, it seemed everything might work out well, but there were still aspects of his personal life that would occasionally drift over into football, with the odd late appearance for training but a rift with Book seemed inevitable at some stage and sure enough, before the 1974/75 season was out, Marsh was again sailing into troubled waters. Book and Marsh were like chalk and cheese in their lifestyles. One was a quiet, thoughtful family man. The other was a seventies superstar with a playboy life outside of football and something had to give. When Marsh was substituted during the final match of the campaign at Luton, it was the straw that broke the camel's back. Plus Marsh was denied permission to travel to watch his old mates from Fulham, particularly his great friend Alec Stock, play in the 1975 FA Cup final because City were to fly out to Nigeria for a tour. It had been a sequence of small disagreements, but it had built a head of steam and a parting of the ways looked the likeliest outcome. However talks in the summer surprsingly led to a new contract being signed

A few months into the following season and City put Marsh on the transfer list. Tony Book said, "I feel Rodney Marsh could have given the club a lot more this season and I think a move is in the best interest of the player, myself and Manchester City."

The catalyst, it seems, was a 0-0 draw with Burnley at Maine Road, when Book's assistant Ian MacFarlane dished out the most severe bollocking Marsh had probably had in his entire career. He called his efforts a disgrace and questioned his commitment to the club. Marsh was angered by Book's decision saying, "I might not be surprised personally but I am professionally. We are currently the most consistent side in the country. You don't expect a transfer when you are captain of such a team."

The one thing Marsh did have was the support of the fans and in the ensuing weeks, protests against their hero leaving began and graffitti was even daubed outside Maine Road in plain view of Book's office. A sackful of mail arrived demanding Marsh stay, but Book had made his mind up and effectively froze the player out of the team. He stripped him of the captaincy and Mike Doyle took over, adding his ten penneth in respect of Marsh.

One thing was for sure – Rodney had played his last game for Manchester City. Fortunately for Book, the team embarked on a 13-match unbeaten run and the furore died down. Marsh was intent on becoming an embarrassment – if necessary – as he sought out a move that was right for him. Fulham were interested, as were Anderlecht. City even went as far as halving their asking price of £90,000 in order to get him out of Maine Road as quickly as possible. Book knew if there were a spate of injuries, he would have difficulty justifying Marsh's absence. He'd already lost Colin Bell for the season, but in late December the move that both club and player had been hoping for came in the form of a £45,000 offer from North American Soccer League side Tampa Bay Rowdies. For Marsh, it was a manna from heaven, for Book, it was a huge relief.

A new life beckoned for the mercurial, if not a little wayward, former England international – the man who when Sir Alf Ramsey warned would "pull him off at half-time" if things were going well replied "Really? At Manchester City all we got was an orange."

The American way was very much the Rodney Marsh way and the sunshine, razzamatazz and cheerleaders complemented his style of football perfectly. He was launched to the supporters aboard a fire engine, sirens blazing, lights flashing – it was the only way he could be introduced, really. A packed stadium went wild and a new hero was born under the name Rod Marsh. After a six-a-side exhibition match, the Rowdies boss said: "If Rod puts a good act together, he'll make a fortune. Entertainment is what I want and he's the man to give it. He's good looking, has oodles of charisma and by golly, he can make that ball talk."

Could he ever!

The gates for the Rowdies were around 10,000 when he first arrived, but within a couple of years, they were playing in front of 50,000 and Marsh's silky skills were the main reason for the dramatic upsurge in interest, and 60,000 would attend his testimonial in 1980.

He had a brief return to English football in 1976, playing for a short while back at Fulham with his old mate George Best alongside him. It was entertainment of the highest calibre, while it lasted, and it reminded everyone what a loss to English football they both were.

Marsh was loved wherever he went because, ultimately, all he ever wanted to do was give the paying customer value for money. Nobody could get people out of their seats like Rodney could and it is a measure of the man that he is still fondly spoken of today, and when the City fans have a good old knees up, you can bet his song will be aired once or twice. Legend? No. Cult Hero? Most definitely – he is the King of Cult Heroes and thank god he stopped by at Maine Road on his royal tour.

Dennis Tueart

1974-1978 & 1980-1983: 269 games, 107 goals

IF THERE'S ONE thing Manchester City fans love to see in their players, it's passion and committment. Throw the odd punch-up, a few spectacular goals and ability and you have all the ingredients for a Cult Hero – and one former City star ticks all the aforementioned boxes – Dennis Tueart. There have been few wingers to stoke the fires of the Kippax in quite the same way Tueart did over a nine-year period, punctuated by a two-year stay with New York Cosmos. He achieved a lot in his time at Maine Road, scoring the winner in a Wembley final, collecting match balls for fun with his knack of scoring hat-tricks and winning a legion of adoring fans, especially the youngsters who idolised him in their thousands.

WEMBLEY WOULD PLAY a big role in Dennis Tueart's career. His name first came to the fore as part of Bob Stokoe's famous Second Division Sunderland team that beat the then-mighty Leeds United in the 1973 FA Cup final, but he'd actually joined the Roker Park club aged 16 after playing for Newcastle Boys, becoming a professional with Sunderland in 1967. He made his debut against Sheffield Wednesday on Boxing Day,

1968. The Newcastle-born Tueart later played his part in the famous victory over Leeds and bigger clubs sat up and took notice, one of them were Manchester City, and no wonder – they'd had personal experience of what he was capable of when he played his part in the 2-2 draw at Maine Road in the FA Cup fifth round tie, not to mention the surprise 3-1 win in the replay as Sunderland powered their way to the final.

The replay defeat virtually sealed the fate of Malcolm Allison who left City soon after and was replaced by backroom boy Johnny Hart. The Blues did reach the final of the 1974 League Cup, but lost to Wolves 2-1, the money gained from the cup run and final, however, financed the biggest-ever payment in English football - £375,000 - as Ron Saunders paid Sunderland £275,000 for Tueart and another £100,000 for Mickey Horswill on the same day.

Tueart said: "I'm delighted to have come to a club who are considered among the best in the country. I couldn't have come to a better club or a better place than Manchester. I've not come down here to taste Lancashire hot-pot."

He made his debut just 48 hours later in a 0-0 draw with manchester United and few doubted that, at 24 and with England under-23 recognition, Tueart was one of the best players outside the First Division. He was joining a team packed with such talents as Denis Law, Rodney Marsh, Franny Lee and Mike Summerbee, though at least three of them were at the wrong end of their careers so there was plenty of incentive to make his mark. "Why should I feel overshadowed?" he said when asked of the household names he would be lining up alongside. "Rodney Marsh, Mike Summerbee and Colin Bell are all tremendous names – fabulous entertainers. I haven't joined City to live in anybody's shadow. I have some ability – and at City they allow you to express yourself."

Tueart only found the net once in his first five games as Saunders' side struggled, and the manager was sacked a fortnight later. He also took part in the 1-0 win that confirmed

Manchester United's relegation a few weeks later but new boss Tony Book was ready to rebuild his ageing side for the 1974/75 season and Tueart would play a major part in the new-look City.

Just two more goals in the first 11 league games of the 1974/75 season suggested the Blues' record signing was yet to find his feet at Maine Road – in fact, including two League Cup ties and the eight games he'd played the previous season, Tueart's record was just three goals in 21 starts. Another 15 games and four goals later, his record was just seven in 36 matches – worse than one every five games, but things were about to change and the Newcastle-born forward was about to haunt his hometown club for the first of many occasions as he banged in his first City hat-trick in a 5-1 win over the Geordies. He ended the season with a very respectable 14 from 39 games and the fans had taken to him and his bustling all-action style.

He was a real handful for any defender and a feisty so-and-so that would land him in disciplinary trouble several times during his Maine Road days. He scored twice more against Newcastle in a 4-0 league win five games into the 1975/76 campaign – he'd now scored five in his last two games against the team he supported as a boy.

He was also, by now an England regular, too and by October, he was also the club's main flair player following Rodney Marsh's spectacular fall from grace with manager Book. Along with teenage winger Peter Barnes, Tueart was flying through the campaign, full of confidence and prepared to try anything to score a goal. The League Cup would prove his speciality tournament as he scored his second hat-trick for the Blues in a 6-1 win over Norwich City. As Colin Bell was stretchered off, his career in the balance, it was Tueart who punished Manchester United in round 4, with two goals in a crushing 4-0 win. The Blues went all the way to the final after seeing off Mansfield Town and then Middlesbrough in a two-legged semi-final, setting up an emotional match against (you guessed it) Newcastle.

Then came the moment that changed his life forever, as Tommy Booth headed a Willie Donachie free kick back across goal and Tueart, with his back to goal, performed a spectacular bicycle kick that stunned the Magpies' keeper and proved to be a fitting winner for City. The name of Dennis Tueart circulated around the world – you don't score a goal like that and fade away into the background and it was replayed from Basingstoke to Brazil a thousand times – no wonder the City fans sung: "Dennis Tueart king of all Geordies!" He'd now bagged six against the Toon in his last three appearances and it's safe to say their fans were heartily sick of him. Everyone wanted to be Tueart in the playground and there were one or two sore backs suffered by young wannabes attempting their own overhead kicks on the bone-hard icy school pitches. Kids tied little white tabs around their football socks and everyone wanted to wear the No.11 shirt. His haul of 24 goals meant he was easily the top scorer in what had been a fantastic season for him.

The arrival of Brian Kidd to partner Joe Royle up front, meant with Barnes and Tueart flying down the wings, City were a handful for anyone. Tony Book had built up a solid team, with a superb defence of Corrigan, Donachie, Power, Watson and Doyle, a midfield of Gary Owen, Asa Hartford, Barnes and Tueart and Kidd and Royle up front. It was a side worthy of the league championship and just one point would separate the Blues and eventual winners Liverpool – it had been that close, and Tueart's return of 18 league goals capped another memorable season for the Blues' dashing winger. But all was not rosy in the garden and when the club made him an offer he could refuse during the close-season, there seemed a possibility he might move on. To lose such a fans' favourite would have been a huge body blow to the club who were preparing to go one better next season and bring the title back to Maine Road for the first time in nine years. City eventually offered terms deemed acceptable and Book said: "This is a contract that commits Dennis to Manchester City for virtually the rest of his career. We are delighted we could reach agreement and both sides are very happy about the new deal."

Yet just a few months later things had turned sour and Tueart claimed the club didn't want him. He was put on the transfer-list in the autumn. It was a curious affair, especially as he'd scored his third hat-trick for City in the second game of the season and there were clearly problems behind the scenes. Said Tueart at the time: "I asked Tony Book if I was wanted or not and all he says is 'maybe, maybe not' and I can't afford a situation like that."

It was hard to believe record signing Mike Channon was the problem as he'd hardly impressed since his £300,000 move from Southampton. The disagreement was hard to understand for the supporters who adored Tueart. He followed in a long line of hugely popular wingers stretching back all the way to the great Billy Meredith – perhaps fans from every club love wingers, perhaps not.

Tony Coleman, Mike Summerbee, Dave Wagstaffe, Eric Brook – great names, fantastic players all loved by the City fans. In later years Peter Beagrie would become a terrace idol – was it possibly because the Kippax terrace used to run the length of the Maine Road pitch? City's home ground was unsusual in that there was no Kop, no behind the goal terracing as such, where the majority of the more vociferous fans gathered. There were occasions when up to 40,000 fans crammed on the Kippax and its two uncovered corner terrace sections.

Wingers would be inspired or shrivel up and fade away at the thought of playing in front of that huge bank of supporters each week and if you didn't have fire in your belly, they'd eat you up. Flair and guts were needed to succeed at City and Tueart had both in abundance – plus he could dine on his Wembley winner for as long as he lives – there can't be a day that goes by without somebody mentioning the goal to him even now. Still, there are worse epitaphs to have!

The problems seemed to have been patched over when Tueart forced his way back into the team and scored yet another hat-trick in a 6-2 win over Chelsea (those were the days!) – his fourth for City and second of the season and five games later, he did it again, a third treble of the campaign as City headed towards the top of the table. His record of 12 goals in 14 games was as good as any in the country, yet six weeks later, he became the second crowd idol to quit Maine Road for America, following the path of Rodney Marsh in a £250,000 transfer to New York Cosmos.

City fans were crestfallen, but the team went on to finish fourth in the table. For Tueart, it was a glamour move to beat all glamour move and the bright lights of New York City beckoned. He'd fallen out of favour with England and had absolutely nothing to lose. The lifestyle, the razzamatazz and the atmosphere of the NASL was perfect for Tueart who thrived on the electricity of the Big Apple and a packed Giants Stadium. Pele had retired but Franz Beckenbauer, Giorgio Chingalia and Carlos Alberto – two of the biggest names in world football – were still there.

Dotted around the country were old mates and former colleagues, too, with Marsh in Tampa and George Best in Los Angeles. They were high times and the City fans kept a keen interest in the progress of their former hero in the form of the odd TV clip and newspaper articles.

They spoke of an exotic lifestyle in a foreign land and the irony was that the Blues were about to crumble from a leading side into shock relegation candidates. Meanwhile Tueart wowed the Americans who loved his style of play and he was soon topping the assist charts as well as scoring for fun.

Regularly playing in front of crowds of 50,000 or more, the football was entertaining and the audience new and hungry. The cynicism of back home was missing and the NASL was not the idyll of the working classes – well, not in the same way. He'd timed his move to Cosmos to perfection and was loving every minute of it.

With an apartment on the banks of the Hudson River, a Cadillac and a $200,000 a year contract, he was mixing with the likes of Brazilian legends Pele and Alberto, socially – it doesn't get much better, does it?

But he had concerns, too. What happened at the end of his three-year deal? He'd be 30 and would he be viewed as the force he once was after so long in a country that were so far off the international radar as to virtually not exist? He knew he had to make hay while the sun shone – and his business acumen could never be called into question. But nothing lasts forever, and around 1979 the American public began to lose interest in soccer. Clubs were folding right, left and centre as crowds dwindled dramatically and the calibre of player moving to the States was nowhere near what it had been a few years earlier as a succession of journeymen footballers – many that had never even made it in England – swamped the NASL clubs.

Tueart could see the future and the champagne had become decidedly flat. He'd miss the days of watching a goal replayed instantly as he trotted back to the halfway line and the board would then flash the message 'Do it Dennis!' or 'Sweet Feet' – ok – this was America...

While he'd had sleepless nights about what lay in store for him once his American adventure was over, there was one club in particular waiting to welcome him home with open arms – Manchester City. After protracted negotiations, including the possibility of a loan deal, the Blues brought Dennis back to Maine Road for his second spell as City player. He could have seen out his time in New York and perhaps even settled there, moving into coaching if he'd really wanted to. But he was ready to come home and home for Dennis, was the city he'd fallen in love with a decade earlier – Manchester.

"Manchester is the greatest football city in the world," he said on his return. "Two big teams, marvellous supporters and rivalry. Injury prevented him making a quick second debut but he was back in March 1980 as City took on Norwich in a 0-0 draw.

In what had been a miserable season, it was just the tonic the City fans had needed and he was afforded a fantastic welcome. His five goals in 11 games – three in the last four – ensured City escaped relegation – it had been money well spent already as far as the supporters were concerned. The team he came back to, however, was unrecognisable. Gone were Doyle, Watson, Hartford, Owen, Kidd and Barnes and Malcolm Allison was now calling the shots with Tony Book taking on more of a general manager's role.

It was, ironically, back in New York that Dennis showed he'd lost none of his passion, desire or tenacity. As City took on AS Roma in a post-season tournament in the Big Apple, Tueart was sent off after defending one of his team-mates. He punched Roma's Maurizio Turone because: "I saw an Italian hit my team-mate, Steppy Stepanovic. Then I felt a tap on my shoulder, I turned around and felt a blow on my cheek. I felt very sick at being sent off."

After being punched himself, he then proceeded to chase the Roma player off the pitch! This was why the City fans loved him – he stood up for himself and others and wearing the sky blue of Manchester City seemed to stoke his fires even more.

The 1980/81 campaign would, however, be a series of highs and lows. Allison and Book were sacked following City's failure to win any of their opening 11 games and John Bond took over the reins. He switched Tueart to a midfield role, perhaps feeling he'd lost a yard of pace to trouble too many defenders and wanted to use his sharp football brain in a more central role. He proved his worth to the new manager by scoring four goals in a 5-1 League Cup victory over Notts County, but was no longer guaranteed a first-team place under Bond. Tellingly, he was left out of most of the FA Cup matches as City made their way to the Centenary Cup final against Spurs and it was perhaps the most disappointing day of his career when he learned he'd been left out of the side to face Tottenham. His experience of playing in major games might just have swung the first game City's way, even as a substitute and he justly felt he'd been snubbed for such a showpiece occasion. He couldn't hide his anger after the game, saying: "I'm very upset to put it mildly. But I don't intend to say anything at this stage that will upset the club. Right now the team is more important than the team." John Bond's reaction was a little disrespectful when he told reporters, "If he wants to go, he can. He's only got to ask for a move and he can have it." Surely he could empathise with Tueart's situation and who wouldn't want to play in an FA Cup final? The fans wanted him to be involved, that was for sure and his name was sung during the first match that ended 1-1.

He climbed off the bench in the replay and instantly made a difference, going close to scoring though Spurs won 3-2. But surpisingly, Bond and Tueart made up and it was clear he did have a future at Maine Road after all. Initially, he was on the transfer list for the start of the 1981/82 season, before some common ground was found between two of the game's strongest characters.

"I seem to have spent my career fighting with managers," admitted Tueart. "Now, at last, I have found one who understands me. The conversations I've had with John Bond this season have been the most invigorating of my career. I believe I have a future with City – but I've had to fight to prove it. What I have had to prove to John Bond is that I came back from America for the right reasons... not an easy ride."

With Trevor Francis joining City in a high-profile move for the new season, Tueart began to play some of the best football of his career, scoring nine goals in 15 league games from midfield. Then, on 19 December 1981, Tueart, with eight goals in eight games, ruptured his Achilles against – of all teams – Sunderland and was ruled out for the season.

It was a crushing blow for City, who two games later topped the table. Without the talismanic Tueart, however, the Blues won just three of their last 19 games to finish tenth. What might have happened had he and Francis stayed fit for the second half of the campaign, nobody knows, but a top five finish must have been a distinct possibility.

The 1982/83 season would be Tueart's last in a City shirt. The fans always felt something out of the ordinary was possible with him in the team and it was his goal in the third game of the campaign against Watford that put the Blues top of the table, briefly, but it was all downhill from there. Elderstatesman Tueart played in 36 of the 42 league games that season, scoring six times along the way. But even the king of all Geordies was powerless to stop City being relegated on the final day of the season in the infamous 1-0 home loss to Luton Town.

Bond had resigned the previous January and there was perhaps too much hope pinned on the 32-year-old's shoulders. With his contract expiring a few weeks later, it was no surprise when the Blues gave him a free transfer. He said: "I feel terrible. I understand the need for economies following our relegation but this is still hard to take."

With temporary boss John Benson soon following Tueart out of the door at Maine Road, supporters wondered why the man who scored 107 goal for the Blues in 269 games hadn't been given a crack as player-manager. He eventually joined Stoke City before returning to Maine Road for a third spell – this time as a director – in January 1993, a position he's held ever since.

A battler, an entertainer and a Cult Hero – what more could you ask for?

Gerry Gow

1980-1982: 36 games, 7 goals

MALCOLM ALLISON'S SECOND Coming was over. He left behind a team stripped of its international stars, bereft of experience with a soft centre that wouldn't hve looked out of place in a box of Quality Street.

The City board, full of ederly men still in awe of Allison the man and too scared to say no to his demands, let it all unfold before their eyes like rabbits stuck in headlines and a side that had touched greatness without actually embracing it, was sold off to finance deals that often defied belief. In just over 16 months, household names such as of Asa Hartford, Dave Watson, Gary Owen, Peter Barnes, Brian Kidd and Mike Channon were sold and replaced by Barry Silkman, Dragolslav Stepanovic, Steve Daley, Mike Robinson, Stuart Lee, Paul Sugrue and Bobby Shinton – and the incoming players cost more than the outgoing stars raised in transfer fees.

Youngsters were brought through and would excel in difficult circumstances, but almost all of Allison's bizarre signings were gone inside 18 months. John Bond had been given the task of saving City, who had begun the 1980/81 season with no wins from their opening 12 games, and his first job was to bring in some wise old heads with plenty of heart, though he had little or no money to spend. He had three men in mind, all of whom would become Manchester City heroes, but one in particular would become a cult hero...

GERRY GOW HAD cut his teeth – legs, head and most other parts of his body – marauding the midfield of Bristol City for the best part of 11 years. His mop of greying curly hair gave him a dishevelled, unkempt look that was entirely in keeping with his image on the pitch. You see Gow was one of football's real hard men. Nobody fucked around with Gerry Gow and if you did, then watch out, because he'd come back and hit you harder and if you were the quarry, you'd better be somewhere else.

His career at Ashton Gate was one of understatement. He got on with his job, got paid and went home. Consequently he became something of a best-kept secret in the West Country, which was just the way they wanted it.

Gow was a hero in Bristol and don't be fooled into thinking he was nothing more than a hatchet man, because it would be doing him a tremendous disservice. He was a ball-winner, yes, but he had vision, was a fine dead-ball specialist, could score goals and worked the engine better than *Scotty* on the *Starship Enterprise*. There was many an opponent when faced with Gow would utter 'I cannae take anymore captain'.

At 28, he'd done all he could with Second Division City and had been criminally ignored by Scotland for the past five years so it was not going to be easy to raise his profile and find a bigger club. But twists of fate at his club and 170 miles in Manchester were about to give him the kind of platform he must have been hoping for for years.

At Maine Road, Manchester City sat bottom of the First Division, a rudderless ship heading for the rocks in treacherous seas. Allison was sacked and his crazed reign ensured that Tony Book went down with him. Chairman Peter Swales knew it would take a manager with proven ability and a big personality to take on what looked like mission impossible and he chose well in Norwich City's John Bond.

Bond was no mug, but he was fed up with life in the quiet East Anglian backwaters and jumped at the chance of managing one of the biggest clubs in the country. Make no mistake, City were at worst on level terms as the top dogs in Manchester back then and only Ipswich Town, Nottingham Forest and Liverpool had enjoyed as much sustained success through the late seventies.

Despite being marooned at the bottom of the league, the Blues still enjoyed an average gate of 33,000 – the potential was frightening. Unemployment was high, but people still wanted to watch football and as we're all aware, a bit of adversity seems to see the Blues' gates increase.

Bond watched from the stands as the team he'd inherited finally found spirit and verve to beat Tottenham 3-1, but the midfield of Tony Henry, Steve Mackenzie, Steve Daley and Paul Power lacked bite and leadership. He also targeted a full-back and a winger and it was these two positions he filled first, signing Bobby McDonald and Tommy Hutchison from Coventry City for around a combined fee of £100,000. Both men played in Bond's first official game in charge, a 2-1 win at Brighton, but Daley's performance in central midfield, alongside the 18-year-old Mackenzie, had not impressed Bond who had a player in mind who would add tenacity and spice to the middle that would hopefully rub off of the rest of the team.

At Ashton Gate, Alan Dicks had been replaced by Bobby Houghton and the new man wanted to generate funds to ignite his side and quickly climb the table. Bristol City had been a respectable outfit during the late seventies, but their star was on the wane and the fact that Houghton was only days into his job meant that Bond's offer of £200,000 for Gow was too good to turn down. Besides, with almost 400 games under his belt and a fantastic return over the years, the club would not stand in his way and the transfer was agreed in time for Gow to make his debut at Maine Road against Norwich and following a few first half rucks and skirmishes it was clear to see that Gow was going to be a huge asset to City's young side.

The Blues took one point out of the next two games, but the Hutchison, Gow and McDonald influence, coupled with Bond's management and tactics was beginning to imprint itself on the side and they won the next three games and drew the next to pull clear of the bottom three for the first time that season and Gow, never prolific throughout his career, scored four goals in four games and his all-action hard-as-hell performances earned him instant idolatry on the terraces.

Each time he left some hapless soul in a heap on the Maine Road turf a chorus of 'Gerry Gow, Gerry Gow, Gerry Gow!' would thunder out from the Kippax.

The fans also fell in love with the other two Scottish signings and both McDonald and Hutchison were huge favourites, but it was Gow who the crowd held closest to their hearts. There's just something special about a ramshackled old Jock wearing a sky blue jersey that stirs the soul of City fans.

The Blues had gone from being a laughing stock and a soft touch to a team that few wanted to play as they built up a head of steam towards Christmas. The Tartan Trio, as they'd become affectionately known as, had all played in the League Cup prior to joining City and were unavailable to play in the competition, but the team was on a roll and the verve and belief that the whole squad now had was evident as the Blues edged past West Brom in early December to win a place in the semi-finals. The supporters didn't know what to make of it all and were agog with the pace of change. Bond was a god and Bobby Mac, Hutch and Gow were already club legends. Two defeats in 15 games – 10 of which ended in victory – was one of the most incredible turnarounds the old First Division had ever seen and the team had already soared into the top half of the table and were as good as safe.

Gow might not have been the skipper, but he led the team in every other sense. He was there to set an example and though his legs were ageing quicker than those around him, he'd put his body on the line and wasn't afraid to get hurt and if somebody didn't like it, he'd stand up to them face-to-face and politely asked them what they were going to do about it. He'd had to fight for this chance and his apprenticeship had been a long and hard one. He'd been a popular figure at Ashton Gate, but to be idolised at a club like Manchester City in such a short space of time must have left him floating on air – if he did the whole floating-on-air thing, which is unlikely.

The FA Cup third round couldn't have come at a better time for Bond's side, who were just about peaking. Seven wins in the last nine and a home draw against Malcolm Allison's Crystal Palace – it had to go with form, and it did, as City won 4-0. In the fourth round, it was Bond's old club Norwich that were put to the sword and Gow's delightful free-kick helped City to a 6-0 victory. A single goal was enough to defeat Fourth Division Peterborough United and then followed an epic quarter-final with Everton.

City trailed 2-1 with seconds left on the clock and 52,000 fans imploring the referee to blow for full-time, but who should scramble home a dramatic equaliser but Gerry Gow to send the travelling fans wild and set up a replay four days later at Maine Road. Gow, Hutch and McDonald were superb as City won 3-1 to make it into the semis for the first time in 12 years and the Blues' support put it all down to the Tartan Trio and the management of Bond.

It was as if all three men had waited all their lives for this one moment in the sun and they were individually all playing out of their skins. They were in an exciting, vibrant team, with passionate fans and a collective will that was surging everyone forward on the crest of a fantastic wave of optimism. They were intoxicating, heady days and the thought of an FA Cup final was, understandably, overshadowing all else.

Following a 2-1 win over West Brom in the league, Gow picked up a knee injury and Bond decided to put cotton wool around two of his talismanic figures, with Gow and Hutchison deemed as 'no risk' category. Gow would not play for a month until he was selected for the semi-final with Ipswich Town, who were strong favourites.

Gow would be up against the Dutch masters Franz Tjissen and Arnold Muhren for the afternoon and it was here that key battles would be won or lost. Barely match-fit and drenched in sweat, it was Gow's tenacity that saw off the more technically gifted opposition and the Blues forced extra time despite several close calls and on 100 minutes, skipper Paul Power scored a magnificent free kick to send City to Wembley.

For Gerry Gow, it was a dream come true – as it was all the team, but it's doubtful anyone deserved it more.

McDonald was popular because he was a capable defender, but it was his goals that set him apart from other defenders at the club – he'd have seven under his belt by the end of the season – not bad in just 36 starts. Hutchison's grace and trickery on the wing made the fact the he was practically unknown by the majority of City fans when he signed close to a crime. He was a beautful player to watch, a Rolls Royce of a footballer who was intelligent and worked hard for the team. He was well into his thirties when he joined the Blues, which is more the pity, because he should have been a huge star and if he'd been perhaps anywhere but Coventry City, he may well have been up there with the likes of Rodney Marsh, Tony Currie and Stan Bowles, such was his ability.

Both McDonald and Hutchison, it could be comfortably argued, were Cult Heroes in their own rights, but in Gow, the fans identified with a player who almost physically embodied their club. As described earlier, Gow's apperance was such that you would certainly notice him, but his passion was mirrored on the terraces, where each fan felt they would have the will and drive of Gerry Gow if they donned the blue jersey. He was pale and the mix of grey straggly hair and Mexican bandit-type moustache gave him a look of any number of blokes down the pub who had run into hard times. The kind who'd knock back a double whisky as though it were a soft drink, light up and then gently tap the glass to order another.

Add to that that City fans have always loved a ball-winner. They love their flair players, too, but somebody who could crunch bones, shed blood and sweat till he dropped all in the cause of Manchester City eclipsed even the great individual talents.

Gow had taken the mantle of Mike Doyle, who'd left several years earlier and it was ironic that he had replaced the man who had possibly kept him out of the Scotland squad for so many years in signing for the Blues – Asa Hartford, though there was still a twist in the tale to come on that particular score. Looking around the midfield of the time and it is clear why Gow was such a favourite. Paul Power was popular but commanded universal respect along the lines of Tony Book and was quiet, unassuming but effective. Tony Henry was a utility player, but had no persona on the pitch that fans could relate to, while Steve Mackenzie was admired and liked because he was still a kid. Steve Daley was just seen as a waste of money and never managed to win over the fans during his disappointing stay at the club. The team and supporters had been crying out for a Gerry Gow for a couple of seasons -they just didn't know it until he arrived.

Gow and Hutchison were both rested for the next three league games as Bond sought to ensure he had his strongest possible team to face Tottenham Hotspur in the Centenary FA Cup final, though both returned to sharpen up in the final home match of the season, a week before the final. Winning the most famous domestic trophy in the world was seen as the perfect postscript to this amazing rollercoaster season that had begun shambolically but was ending majestically. Many believed that it had to be City's name on the trophy and, it probably should have been, but there was to be a cruel twist of irony yet again, just as City seemed to be on their way to victory.

Hutchison's fantastic header had given the Blues the lead and with with just 10 minutes to go, it was still 1-0. But, of all people, Gow lost the ball in midfield and from the resulting Spurs attack and free kick was awarded on the edge of the City box. As the wall lined up, Hutchison overheard Spurs' players intentions and as the ball was touched to Glenn Hoddle, Hutch broke free of the wall to where he believed the ball would be going – he was correct in his guess but his attempt to clear what he believed to be a goal-bound shot ended with a spectacular headed own goal that gave Joe Corrigan no chance whatsoever.

The game ended 1-1 and how cruel that two of the men that had done so much to get City to Wembley should both play a part in giving Spurs a lifeline they'd hardly deserved. The replay ended in misery and was memorable for many things, but the moment an angry Spurs fan breached security to confront Gow over a challenge on Osvaldo Ardilles was perhaps one of football's finest moments. If you have a copy of the replay, put it on slow motion as Gow is booked and suddenly notices this bloke coming towards him from the direction of the stands. It will put you in mind of Robert Shaw in *Jaws* as he describes a shark's eyes as "doll's eyes", meaning they were lifeless and uncaring.

Meet Gerry Gow on his way to defeat in an FA Cup final. He almost goaded the Spurs fan to try his luck but the hapless Londoner was carted away by the police before Gow had the opportunity to ask if his mammy could stitch....

He also probably knew by that time that his moment of glory had gone and may have even felt that there could never be a repeat of the season about to end. As the referee blew for time to signal a 3-2 replay win for Spurs, Gow's time with City was also about to end.

A couple of months into the 1981/82 season, Gow suffered a knee injury that ruled him out for three months and Bond wasted no time in finding an experienced replacement – Asa Hartford. The former City midfielder had been re-signed from Everton and would again represent a formidable hurdle for Gow when he did return from injury, and with the team top of the table going into the New Year, Gow was finally fit and raring to go again. Sadly, despite all he'd done for the club and the fact he'd have been a tremendous asset, Bond decided his future lay elsewhere and encouraged an approach from Rotherham United.

Gow was left angry and hurt by his treatment. He'd battled hard to return to fitness to complement the Blues ascent to the top and yet he was being discarded with little or no respect. The supporters had no say as a deal was done quickly and quietly. Tommy Hutchison would leave a few months later and for many it indicated that the pair had been signed purely as a patch-up job with one season in mind. If so, it was tremedously disrespectful to two of the most popular players of that era and in Gow's case, just a poor decision – there wouldn't have been many opposition midfields that would have enjoyed a 90-minute battle with Gerry Gow and Asa Hartford in direct opposition.

Gow only played 36 times for City, yet he's still fondly remembered to this day and in the mid-Nineties, this writer interviewed Hutch, Bobby Mac and Gow in successive issues for the official Manchester City magazine and then helped arrange a reunion at the Prestwich and Whitefield supporters branch. There wasn't a seat left in the house as the City fans finally got to say a proper thank you to the three men from north of the border.

And what became of City on Gow's absence? Four wins out of the final 20 games saw them slip from first to tenth in the table and Aage Hareide and Graham Baker proved inadequate replacements as City's condition returned to the pre-Bond state – that of catatonic and gradually they slipped towards the inevitable. Bond quit in February 1983 and the Blues were relegated on the final day of the season by Luton Town.

Could anyone have imagined City a) being in that position in the first place with a fit Gerry Gow in the side or b) losing such a crucial game with him in the middle?

The truth is Bond let him go way too soon. He was still only 29 when City sold him and had another three good years left in him at the very least, yet instead was shipped off to South Yorkshire in the footballing wilderness of Rotherham.

Keeping Gerry Gow might just have saved City fans a lot of heartache throughout the Eighties, which were something of an abomination for the Blues. He might even have gone on to player-manage the club had he stayed.

Alas, we'll never know, but what we do know is, you'd want a man like Gerry Gow fighting alongside you in the trenches and when it comes to Cult Heroes, he deserves his place right up there with the best of them.

Trevor Francis

1981-1982: 29 games, 14 goals

JUST TWO YEARS prior to Trevor Francis signing for City, Steve Daley had become Britain's most expensive player having joined the Blues from Wolverhampton Wanderers for £1.47m. Francis had been the first-ever £1m player when he left Birmingham City for Nottingham Forest and not long after, the likes of Andy Gray, Frank Stapleton and Garry Birtles – the latter two having joined Manchester United – moved on for seven-figure fees. There was a battle going on to be the biggest fish in the pond and City chairman Peter Swales wanted in. His thirst to take his club out of the shadow of Manchester United was unquenchable and, subsequently, there were times when he got a little carried away. When manager John Bond said he wanted Francis to take City to the next level, Swales, knowing the move would cripple the club financially, just couldn't help himself. One way or the other, he'd find the money to bring Francis to Maine Road and, two games into the 1981/82 season, he got his man at a cost of £1m. Francis would later claim that Swales was like a man who went into a car showroom intending to buy a Jaguar, but came out with a Rolls Royce and everyone knew what he meant. Ten months later, Francis was gone, sold to keep the club afloat... but what a ten months!

THERE HAVE BEEN some incredible signings by Manchester City over the years. Some of the time, the supporters didn't know what they were going to get and there wasn't a great deal of fuss when certain signings wee announced – think Billy Meredith, Bert Trautmann, Mike Summerbee, Franny Lee, Colin Bell and Georgi Kinkladze. Others caused plenty of excitement – think Peter Doherty, Rodney Marsh and Nicolas Anelka, but Trevor Francis probably just about eclipsed the lot, causing near hysteria for a while as the City fans caught 'Francis fever.'

The Plymouth-born striker had joined Birmingham City as a teenager and made his debut for them aged 16, scoring four goals in one game during his first season. Nottingham Forest made Birmingham an offer they couldn't refuse and Francis became the first million-pound player in Britain. He enjoyed great success with Forest and at the time he joined City, he was at the top of his game and regarded as one of the best strikers in Europe and now he was joining Manchester City. For the supporters, it almost seemed too good to be true, but the club had every right to treat itself after two epic matches with Tottenham in the Centenary FA Cup final just four months earlier. One would have thought the gate receipts from a combined gate of the 192,500 fans that attended the two Wembley finals the previous May would have netted the Blues a tidy sum. It seemed so, as a deal for the England striker moved apace with all parties seemingly eager for the deal to go through.

At 27, the England international could name his price when it came to wage negotiations and he agreed a deal that would net him £2,000 per week to make him one of the highest paid players in England. He penned a three-year deal, despite Brian Clough's attempts to keep the player at the City Ground, ultimately, money talked as it always did and still does. Forest knew that the player's contract was up at the end of the season and decided to cut their losses and while Francis had been sidelined for six months the previous season, he had scored two goals against Southampton on the first day of the 1981/82 season and proved he was fully fit and back to his razor-sharp best.

John Bond was pleased as punch to have landed a truly world class striker and said of his capture, "Trevor is the player we really wanted," he said. "I wanted to surround myself with class players an nobody fits the bill better than this player. It's a marvellous feeling to have this sort of talent in the fold. I am just beginning to get the sort of team I always planned for this great club."

For Francis, it was a chance to do what he did best, score goals. Clough had played him in midfield and he'd lost his England place in the process. West Brom had agreed a fee with Forest as well for Francis, but when Bond told him he'd be playing as an out-and-out striker, he signed for City.

"I know this will be a good move for me. I still have plenty of ambition and all I want to do is score goals and help City win trophies." It was all standard stuff and everybody was saying what was expected of them, but it wasn't hard to see why the City fans were so excited. Francis had electric pace, was a clinical finisher and had excellent vision – he was also a classy act, very easy on the eye with all the style of a Rolls Royce. He'd scored goals for England and got the winner in the European Cup final so he'd proved himself and then some. Following several high-profile striker flops over the past few years, here was a player who surely couldn't fail.

City had begun the season with a win and a draw and were next away to Stoke – the demand for tickets was incredible and whereas there might have been a couple of thousand travelling fans going down to the Victoria Ground, for safety reasons, Stoke pretty much told the Blues they could have as many when it became clear that thousands now wanted to witness his debut. When Francis walked out for the first time as a Manchester City player, he was greeted by 10,000 of his own fans, just 5,000 less than Stoke had, all desperate to see their new hero – and he didn't disappoint, scoring twice in a 3-1 win. It was a thrilling start and the supporters went home in high spirits, looking forward to watching their new hero on home turf.

There were more than 42,000 crammed in at Maine Road for his home debut a week later as City took on Southampton and drew 1-1. Something of a snowball effect had begun, but as if a portent of things to come, following a magnificent display that helped down Leeds United 4-0, he tweaked his ligaments in a nasty clash with Leeds' keeper John Lukic as he laid on a goal for Dennis Tueart and was ruled out for six matches. If ever there was immediate proof that City had almost overnight, become a one-player team, the run of results during his absence – six games, three defeats, two draws and just two goals, suggested exactly that might happen.

The City fans – and it seems the players – were desperate for Francis' return and when he did play again, the Blues beat Middlesbrough 3-2 and then followed it up by whacking Swansea 4-0. Two more wins in the next three games took the Blues into the top four in an incredibly congested top division with Liverpool to come on Boxing Day. Every City fan knew Anfield was the Blues' traditional graveyard and victory hadn't been tasted there for more almost 30 years. On none of those previous occasions, however, did Trevor Francis lead the line and though he didn't score, he tormented one of the best defences in the land all afternoon and an inspired City left with a 3-1 win.

The supporters were in dreamland and really believed the Blues had a chance of winning the title and when Francis scored a fantastic goal against Wolves just two days later in a 2-1 win, City went to the top of the First Division. It had been an amazing first half to the season, but could the team keep it up? Dennis Tueart, who'd been flying with Francis alongside him and scored nine in 15 league games had by this time been ruled out for the season with injury, but the Blues went into the New Year as top dogs and won one and drew two of their next three games. Francis had by now scored 11 goals in 18 games, but a 4-0 win over Brighton in mid-February would be the last truly enjoyable moment of the season and the games thereafter were the beginning of a spectacular anti-climax, even by City's standards.

Tommy Hutchison had left and Gerry Gow was long since gone and the squad was looking painfully thin and there was no money available for reinforcements. In fact, there were suggestions Bond would have to sell to steady the ship. Vultures had begun flying over Maine Road with Francis the target. Southampton offered Steve Williams plus cash, West Brom offered former City favourite Gary Owen plus cash – Manchester United even got in the act, with a cash plus misfiring Garry Birtles the least attractive of all the suggested transfers. All were told Francis was not for sale, but behind the scenes, the board were increasingly concerned at the club's financial plight and there was even a point when Francis's wages weren't paid for several weeks. Fortunately, Francis was so rich it was a while before he realised. The club was quick to amend the situation.

While the team began to stutter – just one win in six attempts, though only one of those games was a defeat – there were signs that the relationship between Francis and Bond was beginning to strain a little. In March, following Francis picking up an injury while playing for England, he was absent for a couple of games, though was selected to play for his country as he neared fitness. Bond warned Francis that he couldn't expect to play for England before he'd played for City and though there was no fall-out, the team's form was clearly causing frustration.

Francis seemed injury-prone, picking up strains and hamstring injuries in successive weeks and at a crucial stage of the campaign, with Europe still a possibility, Francis played just three times in nine games. Yet the fans clung on to the belief that he'd return and fire the Blues back towards the top of the table and everything would be all right – they had to. The truth was, just as it was for Georgi Kinkladze more than a decade later, Francis was a brilliant player in an ordinary side. He'd almost single-handedly carried the club to the top of the division and he just couldn't do it all on his own. When he perhaps should have rested, he was rushed back, compounding his problems. Bond couldn't afford to have a £1m pound player sat on the sidelines, particularly since he was earning £2,000 a week but despite things beginning to go pear-shaped, Francis never grumbled or gave hints he wanted to move by declaring the old chestnut that he was "flattered" by so and so's interest, as is so often the case when a player wants to add a few noughts to his bank balance.

Far from it, in fact. The Francis family finally moved into their designer home in Cheshire in 1982 and were laying down their roots in the area. On the pitch, however, things were getting much worse and four successive defeats, two of which Francis missed, meant Europe was now no more than a distant dream. A 5-0 home defeat by Liverpool (normal service resumed) and a 4-1 thrashing at Wolves seemed to sap the last remnants of confidence from Bond's ailing sides and something had to give. Francis scored twice more and kept his standards right up to his last game, when he was quite outstanding in a miserable 3-1 home defeat to Coventry. By this time he was far and away the club's most effective weapon and a couple of man-markers were usually assigned to shadow Francis in order to nullify the Blues' only real threat.

City finished tenth after topping the table at the halfway point of the campaign. Francis had scored 14 goals in 29 appearances but the concerns among the City fans were he would never play for the club again. The speculation continued, forcing an official statement with assistant manager John Benson saying in May 1982, "Trevor is staying with this club. The stories of him going did not come from us."

Francis' popularity rose to yet new heights when he then added, "I want to stay here. I signed a three-year contract and I have two years of that left and I am happy here. All this speculation doesn't worry me and I've had it for the past 10 years and have learned to live with it."

Reread that last statement and it's not hard to see why Trevor Francis was very much a cult hero. The City fans have long since tired of players who claim to want to stay when they clearly don't, but the difference with Francis was he could have chosen pretty much any club in the country and walked into their side. Yet despite all the disappointments in his short stay at Maine Road, he'd established a strong bond with the club and clearly loved the adulation heaped upon him by the City fans.

And at least during the summer, the supporters could enjoy the rare sight of a City player, playing for England in the 1982 World Cup in Spain. He scored goals in the group games but couldn't find one in the knockout stages and England bowed out in the quarter-finals.

There was a certain pride watching one of 'our boys' worry the best defences in the world.

In the cold light of day, however, there was no way he could stay. The overdraft was reaching untenable levels and the only player the Blues could make serious money on was Francis. Swales, ever canny, kept the news from the supporters until the bulk of the season-ticket sales were in, then, it seems a story was leaked to the *Daily Mail* that Sampdoria were keen on taking Francis to Italy.

Francis, on holiday in Spain learned of the speculation when he read the paper, and said, "I've been so out of touch with the rest of the world that news of the offer actually appeared in the paper before I knew myself. It came as something of a shock to find out City were prepared to let me go."

News filtered back to the City fans and the reaction was one of resigned disappointment. It had been too good to be true from the word go, but it also signalled the beginning of one of the darkest periods in the club's career. A deal with Sampdoria was quickly agreed and City got most of their £1m outlay back for the now 28-year-old. Francis had enjoyed his time with City and liked both Swales and Bond as men, though he felt he'd been somewhat hoodwinked regarding the team's rebuilding plans and the promise of further top class names never materialised.

Francis decided to keep his home in Cheshire, saying that he might even like to return to City one day. "It doesn't seem possible that just seven months ago I scored one of the best goals of my life against Wolves to put City top of the table.

"We could even glimpse the league title. If that dream had been fulfilled, I wouldn't have left City for anything – even if the club had wanted me to go. I would love to come back and play in England, so why not Manchester City? I didn't want to leave the club and shouldn't have had to. Manchester is a fantastic city in which to be a footballer."

The club had clearly overstretched itself one too many times and had to bite the bullet and get their finances in order. Francis signed for Sampdoria for around £900,000, meaning that his one season with the Blues had cost, including wages, about £200,000 - money well spent in the eyes of most. His signing sparked incredible scenes from Sampdoria supporters who clearly felt as happy as the City fans had 12 months earlier.

Meanwhile, Bond's budget was limited to bargain buys, loan deals and free transfers and Francis' replacement? The ageing David Cross who, to be fair, did OK, but nobody turned up at Maine Road when he signed, he didn't excite anyone and wasn't in the same league.

The gates began to fall dramatically.

Bond knew there was no future at Maine Road – his hands were tied and there could be only one outcome. Bond quit in January 1983 and City were relegated the following May – would that have happened if Francis had been in the team? Of course not and relegation would cost the club far more than his wages.

What the club did learn was that big-money signings were no longer the way forward. Francis apart, record signings such as Michael Robinson (£750,000), Steve Daley (£1.4m), Mike Channon (£300,000) and Rodney Marsh (£200,000) weren't paying off. Investment in the youth system, better scouting and not so much of a gung-ho attitude in the transfer market was the only way forward.

As for Francis, he remained in Italy for several years, transferring to Atalanta in 1985 before returning to Britain to play for Glasgow Rangers. He would later manage QPR, Birmingham, Sheffield Wednesday and Crystal Palace with limited success.

Managers came and went at Maine Road during the eighties, and most of the time was spent in Division Two, but Trevor Francis never returned to play for the club again, which is just as well – it could well have spoiled the memory of that one fantastic season when, just for a little while, City fans touched the stars and had a truly world class striker leading the line.

Paul Lake

1987-19?: 130 games, 10 goals

ON 28 OCTOBER 2007 Paul Lake celebrated his 38th birthday. Currently working as a physio for Macclesfield Town, he should have been putting his feet up in his Caribbean bolt-hole, reminiscing about a wonderful career with Manchester City and very possibly at least one top European side. With a clutch of England caps and winners medals to recall his playing days with and enough money to never have to work again, he could have relaxed in the sunshine knowing he'd achieved all he set out to do. Of course, that isn't the way things panned out for Lake, a talent so great that he was already being talked of in the same breath as Colin Bell and a footballer who really did have it all.

THOSE WHO SAW Lake in action either compared him to a thoroughbred racehorse or a Rolls Royce – smooth and able to change through gears with a minimum of fuss or running at a canter, safe in the knowledge that he had plenty in reserve to pass the also-rans before the post. His class and versatility led to inevitable comparisons with Colin Bell and though it is too often said that some players have the world at their feet, in this case, it is perfectly true. But destiny would deal the Manchester-born youngster a rotten hand and he would pay a hefty price for the talent he possessed.

Lake, a City fan from birth, joined the club he loved from Blue Star aged 12. He first came to prominence in City's youth team, at that time run by Glyn Pardoe and Tony Book. Both men knew in Lake they had a crowning jewel - and this among a whole team of youngsters that was of an exceptional standard.

From Lake's class of 1985, half-a-dozen raw recruits would go on to enjoy long, fruitful careers including David White, Andy Hinchcliffe, Steve Redmond, Paul Moulden and Ian Brightwell. When Lake scored his first FA Youth Cup goal in the first round thrashing of Tranmere, he'd made his initial inroad into the psyche of the coaching staff.

City's youth team beat Tranmere 7-1 and to prove it was no fluke, they repeated the scoreline over a decent Blackburn Rovers team in the next round, with Lake again among the scorers. Blackpool and Leicester were confidently dispatched before they beat Fulham 3-0 away to progress to the last eight thanks to a couple of Steve Redmond goals and another Lake effort.

The two-legged defeat of Arsenal in the semis set up an all-Manchester final and it was Lake's goal in the first leg at Old Trafford that helped earn a 1-1 draw and nicely set up the second leg at Maine Road. A crowd of 18,164 roared the young Blues on to a 2-0 win – City's first and only triumph in the competition to date.

Now 18, Lake still qualified for the defence of the trophy the next year and scored three more goals along the way to the semi-finals where a third match was needed to separate two evenly-matched teams, ultimately edged by Coventry City. But Lake's disappointment at youth level was being tempered by first team manager Jimmy Frizzell, who had already given him his full league debut three months earlier. The inauspicious surrounds of Plough Lane may not be everybody's idea of a dream start to their career, but the old Wimbledon FC ground and the 5,667 hardy souls that turned up to watch a dour 0-0 draw with the Dons will be etched in Lake's mind forever.

Wearing the No.7 shirt, he gave a good account of himself and he retained his place for the next two games – a 1-1 draw at Norwich and a 1-1 draw at home to Luton – a game in which Lake managed to score. Not a bad start on his first senior appearance at Maine Road and another boyhood dream realised. There was something about Lake that you simply cannot teach players – every time he had the ball, he always seemed to have time and space. It's a natural asset possessed only by those at the very top of their game. The fans took to Lake immediately, firstly because he was home-grown – always a bonus – secondly, he was a Manchester lad, born and bred and, perhaps most importantly, he was a City fan. Like Mike Doyle before him, he was in dreamland and no club in the world could mean more to him than Manchester City. He may not have spouted venom about United as Doyle did, but in his heart, he was no different, though events in the future would guarantee Sir Alex Ferguson would aways have a place in his heart.

The Blues were, however, slipping out of the top flight and Frizzell chose the most experienced eleven he could for the remainder of the season and Lake didn't play again. City were relegated at West Ham on the final day and Norwich City coach Mel Machin was soon drafted in as the new manager.

Machin had a reputation for grooming young talent and, with the financial coffers well and truly empty, he began to shape a new team based largely around the side that had won the FA Youth Cup just two years earlier. Of course, it was the best thing that could have happened at the time and no less than seven graduates of Book and Pardoe's production line would provide the spine for Machin's team and in the fifth game of his reign, Lake was drafted in to play in a 0-0 draw at Shrewsbury Town.

His first four starts had now ended in draws, but successive wins over Millwall and Stoke ended that particular run and Lake had now won a regular place in the team, though Machin would play him in a variety of roles and by the end of the campaign, this was highlighted by the fact Lake had played in 10 different numbered shirts! His versatility knew no bounds and he could have just as easily played up front as he could in central defence. He played in a manner not dissimilar to Ajax's Total Football theory and understood his team-mates' roles perfectly and more often than not, he could play better than they did, anyway.

During his 33 appearances in the league that campaign, Lake was also a key member of the team that beat Huddersfield 10-1 and then leaders Bradford City 4-2 at Valley Parade on an unforgettable evening in West Yorkshire. Lake was majestic at Bradford, who had been enjoying a long unbeaten run and he'd attained cult status almost from the word go.

The 19-year-old star was playing with a poise and attitude that belied his age and he was also a vital cog in both the FA and League Cup runs the Blues enjoyed, reaching the last eight of both competitions only to fall to Liverpool and Everton respectively. In fact, Lake had already caught the eye of the Anfield scouts and for the next few years, they would keep tabs on Lake and constantly be linked with a move for him in the media, though nothing concrete materialised.

The following season saw Lake earn the first of his five England Under-21 caps and, apart from the odd niggling injury, he was inspirational as Machin's team raced back to the top flight with a point at Bradford on the final day of the season. He thought as a professional, but celebrated as a fan would and that meant the world to the man paying his money on the turnstile.

There was almost a tragic end for the talented youngster when a horrific incident quickly unfolded in front of thousands of people as Lake nearly died during the Blues' 4-2 win over Leicester in March 1988. Those in attendance that day will never forget the sight of their hero lying on the Maine Road turf, legs twitching as he began to suffocate after swallowing his tongue following a nasty clash of heads. The club doctor, Norman Luft, effectively saved the youngster's life that day, freeing his tongue with his fingers and watching in relief as the colour of his skin returned from a ghastly blue.

Full England honours beckoned as he began his fourth season with team he'd supported as a kid in Denton and just a month into the 1989/90 season, Lake enjoyed his finest hour as a City player as the Blues thrashed Manchester United 5-1 in the infamous derby at Maine Road. Lake was ecstatic and in every picture of City's celebrations taken that day, it is clear Lake was pumped up and knew what the game meant to the supporters. It meant just as much to him and for the fans, this was the dawning of an exciting new era with Lake set to lead them into the Promised Land. Comfortable at centre-half, full back or anywhere across the middle, fans labelled him the new Colin Bell, but few realised just how closely Lake's path would mirror the man he was being compared with.

He was compared to another legend of Manchester football, when one pundit declared: "This is what it must have been like watching Duncan Edwards," as Lake represented his country at England B level. Machin was sacked after 13 league games that season and Howard Kendall took over but Lake continued to be one of the first names on his teamsheet. By the end of that season, he'd played 31 of City's 38 league games and been pencilled in Bobby Robson's provisional squad for the unforgettable 1990 World Cup in Italy, though he didn't quite make the cut for the final squad. That he didn't was England's loss.

Still only 21, Kendall saw Lake as City's future and handed his young charge the captain's armband for the start of the 1990/91 season – quite an honour considering there were several other strong candidates, all with a wealth of experience under their belts. Colin Hendry, Peter Reid and Niall Quinn could all easily have skippered the side but there were no arguments when Lake, who ironically replaced fellow youth team graduate Steve Redmond in the role of captain, was selected. The first England cap was probably a few weeks away and the future could not have glittered any brighter.

In fact, he was touted as a future captain of his country and City fans steeled themselves for the inevitable big-money raid from any number of suitors home or abroad. Some things never change…

It's also a measure of his popularity that he was the darling of the Kippax despite having the likes of Reid, Quinn, Hendry, Tony Coton and David White. All were firm crowd favourites, Quinn pushing Lake close for the honours of cult hero more than any other. It was quite a team but then again, Lake was quite a player and never underestimated the power of belonging. Lake belonged to Manchester City and Maine Road was his spiritual home. He had stood on the Kippax cheering on the boys just as they now cheered him on. The sky was the limit. Both he and former youth team colleague David White signed new five-year deals, ending rumours of a Liverpool swoop.

Then, three games into the season, on 5 September 1990, Lake went to play the ball after Aston Villa's Tony Cascarino had miscontrolled a pass and his world collapsed. "My foot went down, I went to go with the ball but the foot just stayed where it was and was twisted," recalled Lake. "The whole knee just went." There'd been no contact; it was just an awkward fall. He remembers it as making a kind of "clunk" noise. Few among the 30,199, Maine Road crowd thought it was anything other than a minor knock as he was taken off the pitch, while they still enjoyed the 2-1 win on the night. Initially, he was told it was a twist and that he'd be back in two or three weeks, but he continually broke down in training as he attempted his comeback. The team was doing well in his absence so there was no desperate rush to get him back playing, but Lake himself knew that there was something terribly wrong. Eventually, following further investigation, the correct diagnosis was made and the parallels with Bell's injury were eerie. Lake, with a partly ruptured cruciate ligament, would miss the next two seasons with the injury. Like Bell, fans marvelled at his attempts to regain fitness and the reception he got for the opening game of the 1992/93 campaign against QPR – Sky's first-ever televised Monday night Premiership fixture - was amazing and quite emotional. For those who'd witnessed it, there were echoes of Bell's return against Newcastle on Boxing Day, 1977, though obviously Lake had achieved nowhere near as much as Bell at that point. That he would do one day, it seemed back then, was certain.

Manager at the time, Peter Reid felt having Lake back was like signing a new multi-million pound star. "My only problem is where to play him," enthused Reid. "He can play in midfield or at the back. He is such a gifted footballer that he could play in any position in his overcoat."

Lake was substituted during the match, but back in the starting line up for the trip to Middlesbrough just two days later. Even then he knew his knee was on the verge of giving way, but his desire pushed him on. Playing for that sky blue shirt was all he'd ever dreamed of and he wasn't about to give it up easily. Then, with barely ten minutes on the clock, Lake went in for a block tackle and fell to the ground in agony. He'd severed his cruciate ligament and his career effectively over.

His upset team-mates looked shell-shocked and even the mild-mannered Niall Quinn was sent off shortly after and within five minutes City had conceded two goals. It seemed their minds – and possibly their hearts – were elsewhere. For the travelling 2,000 or so City fans, most knew they were witnessing one of the saddest nights in the club's history.

Lake said: "I twisted the same way I had against Aston Villa. I knew it was serious. All the ligaments had snapped and the coach journey home was the longest I've ever known"

Boss Peter Reid added his sentiments: "Everyone at the club is devastated and our hearts go out to Paul. After going through such an ordeal for two years only to have the same thing happen again is a tragedy.

"I can promise you this, everything that can be done, will be done."

Reid and the club were as good as their word and numerous operations, at a cost of thousands of pounds followed, including a revolutionary ligament transplant in America, but sadly it was all to no avail and Lake would later admit that he perhaps should have called it a day in the weeks following the Middlesbrough game. Easier said than done, though, especially when he was representing the club he'd dreamed of playing for as a kid.

In early 1996, he did retire and confirmed what had been inevitable for so many years. In October 1997 more than 22,062 fans turned out for his testimonial against a full strength Manchester United (at Sir Alex's behest). Fittingly, perhaps, it was the last testimonial ever played at Maine Road and the biggest gate since the early seventies, eclipsing even such club greats as Joe Corrigan and Mike Doyle. It was also an amazing figure considering he'd been out for almost five years. As a mark of respect, Alex Ferguson sent his strongest squad for the match. Remarkably, hours before the game, his first child, a daughter named Lisa, was born in an emotional rollercoaster 24-hour period that pretty much was in keeping with the great traditions of Manchester City.

Two years later and following 16 operations on his knee, and a variety of roles within the club, he ended a 17-year association with the club. It says just how much the club thought of him that they tried virtually every method known to man to try and get him back playing, but ultimately, they all failed.

"The end came when the surgeon showed me X-rays of my leg and told me he had to be honest with me. The bones were so bowed that there was a real danger of crippling myself if I carried on playing."

Lake moved into physiotherapy and he learned to live with the way his career turned out, though it's doubtful he will ever be able to fully accept it. He never moaned or moped around and believes that the original problem in his knee may have dated back to the 4-2 win at Bradford in 1987 – or even back to his junior days when he would sometimes play almost a diozen games in a week.

"At Bradford I was stamped on by a player who was renowned for not being shy when it came to putting his foot it," he recalled. "I had surgery that corrected the problem resulting from that incident, but it wasn't substantial enough and three years later, I was sidelined again.

"But I played too much between the ages of 11 and 16, which was stupid. I was turning out for City, the school, Tameside Boys and Manchester County. I'd sometimes play 10 games a week –

that's storing up a lot of stress but the better you get, the more pressure there is. I sailed through those years, always wanting to get stuck in in the middle of the park. I think I've paid the price for that in later years.

"I always had it my mind that one day I might be looked back upon as City's most capped player, after the likes of Colin Bell. That was a fantasy of mine back in 1990 when I was involved with the World Cup squad. These things flash across your mind and if you have got any ambition and motivation these things are attainable. That is how I felt at that particular time, when I was playing really well and enjoying the game. I felt at the height of my confidence and realised things could go really well. Then I had the injury and it was all curtailed. I try to look at the positives, though.

"I signed up for Adidas at the same time Paul Ince did when he first signed for Manchester United. I was the so-called star at Manchester City but as Paul's career went from strength to strength, mine just went downhill.

"There are certain names, certain images and certain games that make it hard, but the one thing which really helped me through was the help I had from the City fans. You would not believe it.

"It doesn't take one player to make a team, it takes far more than that. People wondered if I would have still been with City by the time the club slipped into Division Two, but I was a bit like Matt Le Tissier in that there was only one club for me."

He said at the time he reluctantly announced his retirement, "This is the worst day of my life but it is not the end of the world. Nobody could say I didn't give it my best shot." Nobody ever would. Lime a supernova, his star shone with intense light for a short time before blinking out in the night sky. His place in the club's history is assured, but it should have been so much more and while he was a legend-in-waiting, he most certainly attained the status as Cult Hero.

Ian Bishop

1989, 1999-2001: 122 games, 8 goals

DURING HIS TIME as an Everton junior, the story goes that the long-haired Ian Bishop caught manager Howard Kendall's eye for all the wrong reasons. "Get your haircut," ordered Kendall. Whether Bishop lopped enough off is open to debate, but it's safe to assume that Kendall's reservations about Bishop didn't stop with his hair and his next line might as well have been "and pack your bags, you're off to Carlisle."

"Great," replies Bish, "who are we playing?"

"Dunno, son. Ask your new manager."

Of course, it might have been far more amicable than that, but considering the future would conspire to ensure player and former manager would cross paths again, it's entirely possible that Kendall just didn't rate Bishop – or his hair. Either way, Kendall was on a loser and his decision to allow Bishop to leave Manchester City, would lead to mistrust and repressed anger from the City supporters and believe me, as a Harry Enfield character used to constantly say, "you don't wanna do that." Ever.

IAN BISHOP WAS style personified and he was one of England's most underrated players for more than a decade.

While talentless nobodies were selected (from a hat?) by the likes of Graham Taylor and company, Bishop practised his art – and it was art – for a few months with Manchester City and nine seasons with West Ham United. While Carlton Palmer and Geoff Thomas represented their country, Bishop never received so much as a sniff. But then again, he'd spent much of his career having to prove people wrong.

An Everton youth product, he made his debut as an 18-year-old, coming on as a substitute but would never play first-team football again at Goodison Park. A year later he was shipped out to Crewe for a month and part way through the 1984/85 season, he was allowed to join Carlisle United for a token fee of £15,000. He remained at Blundell Park for four seasons and did his job without causing too much fuss. His style of play wasn't really suited to the lower leagues, but he did well enough to represent Carlisle 132 times before Bournemouth manager Harry Redknapp took him down south for the first time in his career for just £35,000. Now Redknapp has his flaws, like everybody else, but he can certainly pick a midfielder and has a list as long as his arm of supremely talented playmakers who have served under him – Joe Cole, Frank Lampard, Eyal Berkovic... the names roll off the tongue and add to that list Ian Bishop. It was a match made in heaven and Bishop didn't have to worry about the length of his hair with Redknapp in charge – he was only concerned with what he could do on the football pitch. In fact, long hair was probably a pre-requisite of playing for Harry, who liked his players to have style, panache and bucket loads of skill. Bournemouth were enjoying great success and were in Division Two along with the likes of Leeds, Chelsea, Birmingham City, Blackburn Rovers, Portsmouth and, of course, City. Bishop quickly became a crowd favourite at Dean Court and along with experienced team-mates like Luther Blissett, they caused one or two teams a a problem or two. In May 1988, the Cherries, as they were known, travelled north to a sun-soaked Maine Road to play the Blues.

A promotion party was planned and the champagne was on ice. City needed two points to guarantee their place back in the top flight and their three previous meetings with Bournemouth had ended in two 2-0 victories and a 1-0 success, so there seemed little to worry about. A total of 30,564 fans turned out intent on enjoying the afternoon, and by half-time, it was game set and match with goals from Trevor Morley and a couple from Paul Moulden giving City a 3-0 lead. Even the Blues couldn't blow this!

But if supporting Manchester City FC teaches you one thing, it's never say never. The next 45 minutes defied belief. Bournemouth fought back to 3-1 – no big deal. 3-2 – er... and then the game went into injury time. The midfielder with the long hair who inevitably drew several loud wolf whistles during the game was everywhere, pulling the strings, making them tick and, wait a minute, haven't 97 minutes been played? They had indeed and, of course, in that final minute, Bournemouth win a penalty – up steps Luther Blissett... 3-3. Unbelievable. Fortunately, there was a happy ending to this story and City got the point they needed with an 86th-minute equaliser in the final game at Bradford City.

City boss Mel Machin had seen enough in the previous game to know who he wanted orchestrating his midfield in the top-flight. So he called Redknapp during the summer asking him to name his price for Ian Bishop and £725,000 did the trick and on 4 July 1989 the cultured midfield maestro became a Manchester City player. The next five months would be extraordinary as the Maine Road express really clicked into gear.

Of his capture, Machin said: "I am delighted Ian Bishop has agreed to join us. Every time we played Bournemouth recently I have been impressed with him and he is the type of player we will need in the First Division."

The relationship that would develop between Bishop and the City fans is best described as a love affair. Sporting a new shorter haircut (apologies to keep going on about it but hair was a big part of Bishop's look) he made his debut against his home city club Liverpool alongside another player destined to become a cult hero, Clive Allen. This was a team that also included another crowd idol in the form of Paul Lake and two other near misses in Colin Hendry and David White – it was clearly a side of crowd favourites, all for different reasons, and to be among their number is therefore even more impressive. Competition was fierce for the affections of the fans.

During the midweek home defeat to Southampton, Bishop received a warm welcome but again found himself on the losing side – but the fans could see he was a quality player and he was like a magnet to the ball.

The moment that Bishop really became a Cult Hero was just three games into his City career and it came at home to Tottenham Hotspur. Paul Gascoigne was up to his usual tricks and went around the pitch, an odd mix of genius and mugging buffoon, intent on taking the piss out of Paul Lake, suggesting he had big ears. Then, it happened – Gazza got his comeuppance as Bishop picked the ball up just outside the Spurs box with Gascoigne challenging him. A delightful dummy and a nutmeg later and the Geordie midfielder was suitably chastised. A roar went around the ground just for that one moment and from the back of the Kippax came a guttural, spontaneous first airing of "One Ian Bishop! There's only one Ian Bishop!" He looked like he'd always played his football in the top flight and the fact that he hadn't was a bit of a mystery. Are you watching Howard Kendall? A win and two defeats later, Manchester United arrived at Maine Road, both teams in the lower half of the table and United boss Alex Ferguson in danger of losing his job.

The next 90 minutes would be the closest thing to Shangri-La most City fans will ever know as the Blues suddenly became the best team in the world, not in our hearts, on the pitch and the man pulling the strings? Ian Bishop. He couldn't have chosen a better game to have a blinder, as did the majority of the team that day and

David Oldfield and Trevor Morley put City 2-0 up with less than a quarter-of-an-hour gone. But there was so much more to come and arguably the *coup de grace* came when Bishop flung himself at a David White cross to make it 3-0 with a spectacular diving header just before the break. Later, he would provide the perfect ball for White to pick out Andy Hinchcliffe to make it 5-1. The whole team achieved a kind of immortality and Bishop had at last found his spiritual home.

City fans have long loved cultured players. Men who could destroy the opposition but do it by playing football the way it was meant to be played. Billy Meredith, Peter Doherty, Johnny Crossan, Neil Young and even Rodney Marsh – there was a great tradition to be upheld and Bishop was punching his wait. It's hard to think of a player who enraptured the crowd in such a short space of time the way he did and both player and club looked set for a long, happy marriage.

Bishop continued to impress with his clever passing, control and poise and he scored another diving header a week later in a 3-1 win over Luton Town – trust me, heading was not a major part of his game. Things were about to get decidedly shaky for the Blues, however, and three heavy defeats in the next five games, culminating in a 6-0 hammering at Derby County, ended Machin's reign as manager of City. There were whispers that chairman Peter Swales and his board felt Machin wasn't high-profile enough for the top division. Swales liked his managers to be brash and flamboyant and compared with Malcolm Allison and John Bond, Machin seemed dour and boring. The fact that he was a bloody good coach and had earned the right to at least a bit of time to get things right hardly seemed to matter.

Speculation as to who would be the next man in the hot-seat raged with Joe Royle, then boss of Oldham Athletic and Howard Kendall, recently returned from a brief spell managing Atletico Bilbao in Spain, the leading contenders. Royle was the first choice and had he accepted the Blues' approach, the destiny of Ian Bishop would have likely taken a completely different route – as it was, the pair would be reunited eight years later at Maine Road. Royle's decision to remain at Boundary Park meant the job was Kendall's, if he wanted it – and he did.

What must Bishop have made of the choice given his past with the former Everton boss. Would time have changed Kendall's opinion of Bishop? Kendall's first teamsheet would give a clue of what lay ahead – and Bishop's name was on it... as a substitute. Taking over Bishop's No.4 shirt would be new signing and player-coach Peter Reid. Things looked bleak and even though he was selected for the next game against Norwich, reports in the press suggested it would be his last game for City. Despite flags and banners protesting about the imminent transfer and the constant chanting of Bishop's name throughout the 1-0 win, he was substituted to a stirring standing ovation, some say with tears streaming down his face. He knew, Kendall knew and a couple of days later, everybody knew. Second Division West Ham couldn't believe their luck as Bishop and Morley were swapped for ex-Everton midfielder Mark Ward. Their hero gone, many City fans vowed never to get behind Kendall for this treacherous act. Selling the club's only creative player and arguably the best at the club on the evidence of the first 18 league games. The calibre of player coming in was clearly dogs of war as opposed to style and grace and the football served up was certainly effective, but desperately dull.

Bishop, meanwhile became a hugely popular figure at Upton Park, helping the Hammers to promotion in 1991 and on 18 April 1992, he returned to Maine Road with West Ham to a hero's reception. Kendall had by this time gone, after he sensed he would never be fully accepted to the Manchester City supporters. Blues fans looked on enviously as Bishop prospered in East London, ironically now under the leadership of Harry Redknapp, the man who had reluctantly sold the player to City in the first place.

Peter Reid was player-manager at Maine Road from November 1991, Kendall having returned to manage Everton spouting some cock and bull story about love affairs and marriage. To be fair, he'd done his job and helped turn City into a top six side, but he was to discover the old adage 'you can never go back' to be true in this instance as things went pear-shaped at Goodison Park.

Things came full circle for Bishop, however, when Joe Royle returned to manage City and, on learning the midfielder was available on a free transfer, he brought him home to Maine Road. A lot had changed in that time and was effectively replacing the terrace idol of the century in Georgi Kinkladze who was set to join Ajax at the end of the season. The City fans still welcomed Bishop back with open arms, but things could never be quite the same as they were back in 1989. How could they? Nearly a decade had passed and a lot of water had passed under the bridge. Royle described the deal as "too good to miss" and added, "He may be 32, but he is a great passer of the ball and will give us one or two more variations. West Ham have decided to give him a free transfer because of his long service, and that means a very good deal for us."

Bishop was still pinching himself at the move. He said: "I remember playing Norwich and the crowd singing my name throughout the game. Word had got out that Howard Kendall was ready to sell me and there were banners on the Kippax begging me to stay. I cannot describe how that felt – I didn't want to leave City but I knew there was no future at the club.

"Ever since then, I hoped I might one day return, but you wondered if that would ever happen. I never had a moment's hesitation about returning. In fact, I couldn't get over there quick enough.

"I always regretted my first spell only lasted six months – it wasn't enough and every time I returned with West Ham the reception was amazing. Pulling on the City shirt again was a very emotional moment for me."

He made his second City debut the same day as Shaun Goater, the £400,000 buy from Bristol City, though neither player could prevent a 2-1 defeat at Bradford City. The Blues were sliding towards relegation and there seemed little anyone could do about it and on the final day of the season, a 5-2 win at Stoke proved pointless as all the teams above that needed to win did, and City were relegated. Bishop had gone from the Premiership to Division Two in the space of two months! He must have watched as Kinkladze left the pitch to an incredible ovation from the thousands of travelling City fans and it must have stirred memories of his own departure back in 1989.

Pitted against Kevin Horlock, Jamie Pollock, Danny Tiatto and Michael Brown for the midfield spots, Bishop's role in his 'second coming' would be less than he'd imagined, particularly as City struggled throughout the first half of the campaign, arguably bottoming out with a 2-1 at York that left them halfway down the table. Bishop was subbed in that game and a watching Shaun Goater said, "I couldn't believe it when Joe brought Bish off in that game. He was the only one who made us play football and I just thought 'don't take him off now, Joe'. I remember Bish looked pissed about that decision."

The stop-start nature to his season meant he never really showed his best form as City finally limped towards the play-offs and a hamstring tear meant Bishop was rated very doubtful if the club reached the play-off final. Fortunately, after a closely-fought tussle with Wigan, City did reach Wembley where they faced Gillingham for the right to a place in Division One – Bishop just about won a place on the bench after convincing Royle of his fitness. Bishop came on as a sub to replace Michael Brown with the score 0-0 and, at last, City began to stroke the ball around and, of course, they would eventually triumph on penalties after an incredible match.

With the pace a little less frenetic in Division One, Bishop reclaimed his first-team spot and rolled back the years with a series of inspirational midfield displays. He was back to his best again and was conducting the orchestra to play his tune. When Leeds United, then a major Premiership force, took on City in an FA Cup tie at Maine Road, Bishop scored a spectacular half-volley that fairly sizzled into the roof of the net to give the Blues the lead. It was just like old times again.

He remained in or around the side throughout the 1999/2000 season but was on the bench for the final match at Blackburn Rovers, where only a win would guarantee a most frantic return to the Premiership. With City trailing 1-0 at half-time, and lucky to be still in the contest, Royle brought Bishop on and immediately, the Blues looked a different team. They won 4-1 and Bishop was magnificent. His dream of playing in the Premiership with City was going to come true, though the pitch invasion of around 15,000 City fans left the claustrophobic Bishop in a state of panic, though he eventually made it to the players' tunnel.

Life in the Premiership was tough for City, however, and Royle used Bishop sparingly and his substitute appearance during a 3-2 win over Birmingham City would be his last for the club before jetting off to play for Miami Fusion in the Major Soccer League. He'd done his job by helping City back to the Premiership and who could blame him for swapping an occasional spot on the bench for a glamorous life in the States?

After a year, though, Miami went bust and Bishop returned home to play for Barry Town who were about to play in the European Cup – at 37, he'd finally made it! Of his time in America, he said: "I drove to training on a Harley Davidson wearing a T-shirt and shades. At the front of my house there was the Atlantic Ocean and at the back it was like millionaires row, with lots of little canals with luxurious boats chugging up and down."

He stayed with Barry before turning out for Rochdale for a spell and then Radcliffe Borough. He ran a pub in Southport for a few years before jetting back out to America to take up coaching. A wonderful player that City fans caught only a glimpse of at the beginning as well as something of a cameo role at the end. Arguably, they never saw him at his peak and if he had remained with the club, we'd instead be talking about a Manchester City legend. A true Cult Hero if ever there was.

Clive Allen

1989-1991: 68 games, 21 goals

THE EIGHTIES HAD been a succession of disappointments for City and a particularly hard time for the loyal and still sizeable hardcore following the Blues enjoyed. It had begun with the spectre of relegation hanging heavy over the club in 1980/81 before an amazing recovery, thanks to the sacking of Malcolm Allison and arrival of John Bond, led to a tenth-placed finish and the 1981 Centenary FA Cup final. Had City won that game, who knows what might have happened over the next decade? As it was, the Blues were relegated in 1983, promoted in 1985, then relegated again in 1987 before returning to the top flight after another two-year absence, in 1989.

The strikers leading the line from 1983 to 1988 ranged from the raw to the ridiculous. An array of forwards, many Scottish and well past their sell-by date, joined the cash-poor Blues and sometimes, they even made a decent fist of it.

Former Rangers and Leeds striker Derek Parlane enjoyed an Indian summer with City during the 1983/84 campaign and his partner up front Jim Tolmie, the diminutive former Morton 'star' (do Morton actually 'do' stars?) shone briefly, too, but the three Gordons – Dalziel, Davies and Smith, didn't. Tony Cunningham and Jim Melrose were chalk and cheese and Mark Lillis tried his hardest during a brief stay. Chris Jones and Trevor Christie might as well have come on the pitch in Zimmer frames, such was their ineffectiveness – that plus the fact they both had mullets of varying degrees. Imre Varadi and Paul Stewart were productive, and minor cult heroes to boot, but it was the goals from homegrown David White plus a few from Northampton Town capture Trevor Morley that won promotion in 1989.

It was a testing time to be a City fan and Mel Machin, the Blues' manager back in '89, knew he needed a proven goalscorer to lead the line if his young team were to avoid a quick return to Division Two. His current main striker, Wayne Biggins – an honest, but journeyman footballer - was hardly likely to trouble the defences of Liverpool and Arsenal. Machin knew exactly who he wanted and was prepared to gamble a large percentage of his transfer budget to bring him to Maine Road. He thumbed his French phrasebook as he picked up the telephone, but it wasn't some European hot-shot he was targeting – more an English scoring past-master.

CLIVE ALLEN HAD done the rounds, but like the milkman, he had always delivered for his employers. Born in Stepney, London, on 20 May 1961, his father Les had been a member of the legendary Tottenham Hotspur team which won the First Division title and FA Cup double in 1961, becoming the first club to achieve this distinction in the 20th century, and his dad helped secure the FA Cup triumph exactly two weeks before Clive was born. Part of a rich football dynasty, Clive is the brother of Bradley Allen and cousin of both Martin Allen and ex-West Ham United and Spurs midfielder Paul Allen.

Clive began his career with QPR, then joined Arsenal for just 62 days during the close season, never kicking a ball before being whisked off to Crystal Palace in a player-exchange deal with Kenny Sansom. He then returned once more to Loftus Road to further enhance his reputation. But it was with Tottenham that he became something of a household name as a lethal goal poacher, being very much in the same mould as another Spurs legend, Jimmy Greaves, who, hardly surprisingly, was Allen's idol. Indeed, Greaves enjoyed some of his best years at White Hart Lane, but was immensely proud that it was Allen who broke his record with a spectacular haul of 49 goals in one season during 1986/87 (for the record, that's 13 goals more than the entire City side of the same season managed to score in their 42 league game programme). It was hardly surprising that he collected the PFA Player of the Year and the coveted Football Writers' Association Player of the Year awards that same season.

In 1987 Allen decided to try his hand abroad, joining French champions Bordeaux for 18 months. It didn't quite work out for him there (it is a measure of his success that 'didn't quite work out' equated to 14 goals in 19 games), however and he was eager for a return to England. When Manchester City lodged a £1.1m bid for the 28-year-old, Bordeaux accepted and, for the first time in his career, Allen would ply his trade north of Watford.

IRONICALLY, ALLEN COULD have been a City player for perhaps a decade by this point, but he picked up a slight injury while having a trial at Maine Road as a 15-year-old. Despite things not working out for the teenager, he remembered the club fondly as he recalled: "I opted to join QPR in the end, but the funny thing was, physio Roy Bailey and chief scout Ken Barnes were at Maine Road back then and when I actually signed for City in 1989 they were both still there! I'd always had good vibes of the place because I'd been there as a kid and I was delighted when City came in for me."

Incredibly, he was the club's first £1m-plus signing since Trevor Francis way back in 1981 and, for City fans, Allen represented a major step in the right direction. It meant the club could once again compete with the best and for many, Allen's willingness to come to Maine Road was an endorsement that good times were just around the corner again. He had the backing of the crowd from the moment he arrived.

Most importantly, Machin understood what made Allen tick and of his new signing, he said: "He's scored close to 200 goals in little more than 300 senior appearances. I don't believe there is anyone playing today who can match that record, not even Gary Lineker.

"That is why we've brought him here and it will be my job to make sure that he gets the service he needs. I don't want him making saving tackles in our penalty area. I want him where he is at his most dangerous – in front of our opponents' goal. It staggers me that he scored 49 goals in one season when he was playing up front on his own."

Indeed, Allen's career-scoring record was exemplary and he was the perfect choice to partner David White, David Oldfield or Trevor Morley, though neither Allen nor Morley would worry defenders with their pace. White was raw pace and energy but could frustrate with his finishing; Morley was industrious, but never prolific and Oldfield might have had a decent turn of speed, but he looked lightweight and was never clinical.

All Allen needed was opportunities, perhaps one or two good ones during 90 minutes and he'd stick the ball away – there was nothing surer. He made his debut in the toughest of surroundings, wearing the No.8 shirt at Liverpool on 19 August 1989 and the Blues predictably went down 3-1. Still adjusting from the somewhat gentler pace of French football, Allen failed to score in any of his first four games and just one point from 12 left Machin's side rock bottom of the table. Allen was either given – or more likely asked, Trevor Morley for the No.9 shirt and wore it for the first time in the 2-1 defeat at Coventry. Typical then, that whilst wearing his favourite shirt for the first time in front of the Maine Road crowd, he should choose one of his former clubs, QPR, against whom to finally open his account for City. A cool finish just inside the box in front of the North Stand fans was enough to win the game 1-0 and take the team off the bottom. Allen punched the air in delight and relief, but he would miss the next three games through injury and among them was the unforgettable 5-1 win over Manchester United. Had Allen played, it's entirely possible the outcome of that game might have been completely different, with his replacement David Oldfield scoring twice on the day.

Following his return to fitness, he was substitute for the first two games before he climbed off the bench to score a spectacular last-minute equaliser at Chelsea. A 6-0 defeat at Derby County two games later signalled the end of Mel Machin, however, and Allen would never again be guaranteed a first-team place at Maine Road.

Machin's cavalier approach to attacking football, not exactly unappreciated by the supporters, had ultimately cost him his job and when Howard Kendall took over, it was clear that the ethos of the team was going to change and everyone was expected to put a decent shift in from goalkeeper to striker. It was back to basics and the team would be based on two solid banks of four players in defence and midfield, with the forwards helping out in defence whenever necessary.

That didn't bode well for Allen, who had made a career out of saving his energy for the opposition's penalty area, with great effect, of course. Kendall's early signings included Alan Harper and Peter Reid and there was a recall to the first team for defensive midfielder Gary Megson – Allen must have wondered where his chances would come from with little or no creativity in what was clearly a 'dogs of war' team. It was especially hard for a player who'd once had Chris Waddle, Glenn Hoddle and Osvaldo Ardiles creating chance after chance for him just a couple of years before at Tottenham. But he'd done enough to initially impress Kendall having scored in each of the three games prior to his appointment. Though he started in Kendall's first match at Everton, a dour but priceless 0-0 draw, he was benched for the Boxing Day visit of Norwich City. He came on to score the winning goal – his seventh strike of the season – not bad for a player with only a dozen starts under his belt. The fans loved

Allen – sometimes the City crowd just takes to a player – there's no rhyme or reason to it, they just like them from the word go and there's no explanation. David Oldfield must have looked at Allen and wondered why he wasn't a terrace idol, too – hadn't he scored twice against United in the Maine Road massacre? Didn't he give his all for the team as well?

Kendall, though, never seemed totally convinced of Allen's worth to the team. He wanted industry and sweat and he instead turned to Wayne Clarke for a while, when Allen's continuing injury niggles kept him out, Kendall signed his fifth former Evertonian when he brought in Adrian Heath. Despite City climbing the table steadily, there was a growing resentment toward Kendall and his negative tactics and especially the number of 'old boys' he'd brought to the club. He'd already sold the hugely popular Ian Bishop and Trevor Morley to West Ham in exchange for yet another ex-Toffee in the form of Mark Ward – and now another firm favourite Allen was under threat with the arrival of Heath. The City fans felt Maine Road was quickly becoming an ex-Evertonian retirement home and it was hard for many of them to swallow – the Manc/Scouse relationship in football has never been anything less than hostile to say the least. Allen was in and out of the team, but whenever he was sub, the fans let Kendall know who they wanted on the pitch.

Niall Quinn was signed towards the end of the season and would have been an interesting strike foil for Allen, but the pair rarely started together. By the end of the campaign, City were safe and Allen had scored 10 times in 23 starts in the league, plus added two more in the League Cup and it's worth noting that he scored home and away against former clubs QPR and Crystal Palace that season.

There was perhaps another reason the City fans took Allen to their hearts. For many, the fact he'd been all but ignored by England, in many ways, embodied a belief (backed with hard fact) that City players never really get the recognition they deserve from England. In the past, Mike Summerbee, Joe Corrigan,

Mike Doyle, Gary Owen, Paul Lake, David White and, later, Keith Curle, all were largely overlooked or never given a real chance to show what they could do for their country.

There was, and still is, a feeling of bias against City, while Manchester United reserve players are regularly selected for national duty. Quite how Allen had won just five caps for his country up to the point he joined City remains a mystery, but it further endeared the striker who liked to play with a smile on his face to the Blue half of Manchester.

Many expected Kendall to ship the last few Machin signings out of Maine Road during the close season, but Allen soldiered on and scored a bagful of goals on a pre-season tour of Sweden in a bid to win over Kendall, but found himself back on the bench for the opening match at Spurs, excluded for the next two games and then sub for the next six matches. By November, Kendall, who despite making the Blues a solid outfit capable of holding their own in the top flight, had quit and returned to Everton, leaving his ageing signings behind, one of which became City's new player-manager – by popular demand - Peter Reid.

The bad news for Allen was he was most definitely not a player Reid wanted leading the line in his team. Rumours of a training ground spat between player and manager refused to go away and Allen found himself out in the cold with his days at Maine Road numbered. Yet there seemed a glimmer of hope when, with City being held by lowly Port Vale in a fourth round FA Cup tie, Allen told Reid to put him on for a just-won corner and promised he'd score the winner. Calling his bluff, Reid sent Allen on to a raucous welcome from the travelling support and he still seemed to be adjusting his kit when the ball came across and, like a magnet, went directly to Allen who sent a bullet header into the net for a dramatic winner, just as he'd predicted. He just had that uncanny knack of being in the right place at the right time – an almost unteachable skill borne almost completely from instinct. Reid later claimed: "Clive said he'd get me a goal and was as good as his word. I'll never doubt him again." But after a brief run in the side, he left him out again and resentment grew against the man the fans believed was taking his place – Adrian Heath – who would complete the season with just three goals in almost 50 appearances. Heath seemed to get under the noses of the Blues' fans, who saw him as no more than Reid's mate and his ineffectiveness in front of goal made many wonder exactly what his role in the team was. Allen had scored four times and had just eight starts that season – it wasn't hard to understand the fans' thinking, but falling out with the boss is never a good idea, no matter how lofty your reputation is and Reid wanted him out. The truth was Allen was an embarrassment to Reid, a constant source of debate among the supporters who, when things were going badly for those who did start, questioned his managerial judgement. But if he'd hoped Allen would just fade away and quietly and leave City, he was wrong and when he set up a deal to take the player to Luton Town in the close season of 1992, Allen informed his boss he would rather stay at Maine Road and fight for his place.

"I don't know whether it was down to his inexperience as a manager but I should not have been treated in the way I was by Peter Reid," said Allen, now a coach at Tottenham. "I trained with the kids for 10 weeks - Garry Flitcroft, Michael Hughes, Mike Sheron and several others who were there at the time - and all this because he wanted me to leave and I wanted to stay and fight for my first-team place.

"He never spoke to me in that time and held it against me that I went against his wishes. There were some painful times, but after three or four weeks I just thought 'what the hell? I'm going to tough it out and see it through. I can play for whomever I want!'

"The fans gave me support whenever they saw me. I feel closer to them as a set of supporters than I do with any other club. I felt City was the right club for me, but the manager wouldn't speak to me for weeks and weeks. I was not a Howard Kendall type of player either, but at least he made me feel wanted and part of the squad. I didn't get any of that with Reidy."

The move would have brought in much-needed funds to finance other deals for Reid and the manager was angry that he'd been unable to offload the former England man after thinking it was a done deal with Luton. Forced to train with the youth team and play reserve team football for the first three months of the season, an injury crisis meant Reid had no option but to recall his rebel star. Well, it was either that or explain to 35,000 supporters and an angry chairman and board why one of the country's most prolific scorers was idling away with the reserves - and he was named as sub for the trip to relegation favourites Notts County. Allen recalls the time with crystal clarity: "One afternoon, I think it was a Friday, I got a call from Sam Ellis saying I was to report to Maine Road on Saturday morning. I was in the squad for Notts County - I was suddenly back in the frame.

"I turned up at the ground and the banter was flying about, which was great. Gary Megson turned round and said 'who's the new player?' and everyone had a laugh.

"The media picked up quite quickly on the situation and hyped up my comeback. The travelling thousands gave me a great reception, something that I'll never forget.

"I came on as a sub and my first shot was handled on the line. We got the penalty and Steve Redmond, I think, was the penalty taker still at that stage - although Reidy took one at Leeds and missed and might've fancied it again. 'Reddo' picked up the ball and I was right next to him. He looked at me and said 'Do you want to take it Clive?' I grabbed it off him and said 'Yes indeed!'

"I remember when I saw it hit the back of the net that I'd never experienced such a feeling of relief and joy all at the same time. I'd had to keep all that anger and hurt to myself for 10 long weeks. I'd kept a dignified silence, but I knew eventually, one way or another I'd have my say and I was having it then.

"I kissed my badge and ran over to the City fans. Literally 90 seconds after the restart I connected very sweetly with a cross from the right and buried a volley right into the bottom corner and I can tell you that goal meant so much to me.

"Again it was over to the City fans – by now I'd been on the pitch four minutes and scored twice! I scored again in the midweek League Cup-tie against Chester and the City fans shouted: 'Are you Watching Peter Reid?'"

It would prove to be a pivotal moment in the relationship of manager and player, Reid had finally bowed to the constant chanting from the travelling City fans and sent Allen on but in a war or attrition, sprinkled with simmering hostility, he'd actually shot himself in the foot – wasn't this what everyone had said would have happened if Allen had been playing?

Reid had been the first to greet Allen as he ran off to celebrate, Allen pushed him away and a heated exchange followed as striker ran to the ecstatic City fans and kissed the badge on his shirt – and this at a time when few ever did such a thing. The anger and frustration had become very public and there could be only one winner after this and it wouldn't be Clive Allen. When he did return to fitness following his injury lay-off, he was largely ignored, as had been the case before. Only Reid's own popularity among the City faithful saved him from a severe backlash, though many were still unhappy at Allen's shoddy treatment and never fully forgave him. The dissenters would have their day a couple of years later.

Knowing Reid daren't drop him for the potential banana skin League Cup-tie with Chester a couple of days later, Allen told the *Manchester Evening News* that the Blues' boss was out to ruin him.

He said: "Peter Reid and Sam Ellis are trying to destroy my career, but it won't work. They cannot treat people the way they have treated me for the past 10 weeks and expect to get away with it.

"I am not a nervous 19-year-old who is afraid to speak his mind – the way I've been treated this season is disgraceful. If the two goals I scored at Notts County embarrassed them yesterday then that's fine by me. The manager hasn't spoke to me all season and couldn't even bring himself to say 'well done' yesterday.

"I can accept not being part of his plans, but he has not even had the guts to explain the situation to me. I've never caused the club an ounce of trouble and all I want to do is play for Manchester City."

The comments caused a furore at the club but Allen knew he had nothing to lose. Even chairman Peter Swales felt obliged to say that he thought Allen's comments were "out of character and out of order" – proof, if needed, that he was under something close to mental torture?

He was selected to play against Chester – and scored – but was soon out of the picture again. If three goals in one and a bit games weren't enough to earn a last chance, nothing was. The striker finally accepted defeat and, despite two more brief substitute appearances, in December 1991, Clive Allen joined Chelsea – another club his father once played for – at a cost of just £250,000. The battle of wills was over and Reid had finally won. To be fair, his preferred strike partnership of Niall Quinn and David White was proving to be extremely fruitful, but the master predator was surely worth hanging on to and utilising more often – alas, it wasn't to be. As an indication of just how cheaply City let him go, he would cost Millwall £750,000 from West Ham some two years later. He had a brief spell following a bizarre move to Carlisle before hanging up his boots and becoming an American football player as a specialist kicker for NFL Europe side London Monarchs. It's just a pity he never got the chance to thank the City fans properly for receiving the kind of backing all players must dream of – unconditional.

Uwe Rösler

1994-1998: 177 games, 64 goals

THERE WASN'T REALLY one particular moment that Uwe Rösler became a cult hero – he was sort of one from the word go, and this despite an appalling mullet hair-do – but then, the lad was from East Germany where time had pretty much stood still since the Second World War. Despite his origins, he was a typically English centre-forward – strong in the air, decent on the ground and prepared to work hard for the team. He wasn't particularly quick and though he could hold the ball up well, he wasn't as technically gifted as some of the strikers in the Premiership, yet there was something about him. He wore his heart on his sleeve and stood up for himself, even when times were rocky with a section of the City fans. But ask any supporter who their favourite top five players of the last 20 years has been and Rösler's name will crop up time and time again. Cult Heroes aren't manufactured – they just sort of happen. Uwe was destined to be a huge favourite at Maine Road and if you stand on the patch of ground where the Kippax used to be, on a windy day, you can sometimes still here the repetitive chanting of Uwe Rösler's name to the tune of 'Go West'...

ON NOVEMBER 15, 1968 in Altenburg, East Germany, Uwe Rösler was born. Just six months earlier, Manchester City had been crowned champions of England. At that point, the path of baby and football club could not have been further apart, but of course, this would change a couple of decades later.

In the second half of the 1993/94 season, City knew they were in for a relegation battle and manager Brian Horton was acutely aware that his problems lay up front, where goals were increasingly hard to come by. In the previous 10 games since the turn of the year, just two of the five goals scored had been from a striker – Carl Griffiths and five of those games had ended without his side scoring at all. The Niall Quinn and David White partnership that had served the club so well for the past couple of years came to an abrupt end within the space of a month before Christmas when Quinn damaged cruciate ligaments and White was swapped with Leeds' David Rocastle. With only Griffiths, Sheron and the on-loan Carl Shutt, City were looking decidedly lightweight up front and there seemed every possibility that the lack of goals would cost them their Premiership place.

Horton decided to go for broke – he targeted three forwards that he wanted to bring in before the transfer deadline and was determined to get them all to Maine Road.

The first of the trio was Nurnberg's former East German international Uwe Rösler, who was at the time on loan with Dynamo Dresden. It's safe to say that even the anorakiest of City fans had never heard of the forward and therefore, there was very little expectation as he flew into Manchester for a trial with the Blues. In fact, the move was a complete gamble for Horton who had never seen Rösler play.

"There is no limit on the time he will spend with us," said Horton. "He has joined us on a trial basis, which would then be extended into a loan if he makes a good impression. That loan could become a permanent transfer although at this stage we haven't discussed a fee with Nuremberg."

At 25, he was an experienced international and young enough to be worth taking a punt on, but Horton didn't have limitless funds and knew Rösler would have to look the part if he was to pay good money for a relatively-unknown quantity. He'd started out at FC Magdeburg before moving on to Dynamo Dresden and then Nuremberg but his record of just 26 goals in 130 appearances suggested he was at best a gamble. In fact, Rösler had attracted a notorious reputation in his own country as an over-physical striker with a poor disciplinary record. Horton, however, was desperate.

He arrived in time to make his debut for City's reserves at Burnley and scored two gaols. Three days later Rösler made his debut at QPR – the first German to play for City since Bert Trautmann retired some 40 years earlier – and set up a goal for David Rocastle with a smart back-heeled pass. A 1-1 draw was a decent result and Horton moved quickly to further improve his forward line by signing Paul Walsh from Spurs for £700,000 and a few days before the March transfer deadline, he bought Peter Beagrie from Everton for £1.1m. The trio would transform a shot-shy side into a team with lustre, capable of causing any defence problems.

Both Rösler and Walsh were excellent in the air and in Beagrie, they had a winger supplying them with crosses that were often harder to miss. All three scored in the first home game they played together – a 3-0 win over Aston Villa and following a third successive Premiership win, Horton simply asked Nuremberg, 'How much?'

A £500,000 fee was agreed and Rösler became a City player. His three goals in the last four games meant he'd bagged five goals in eight games and relegation fears had been banished. when he grabbed an equaliser in the final game of the season away to Sheffield Wednesday. The travelling army had a new hero and sang his name on the way back to their cars and coaches.

Rösler said at the time: "I don't really care what they say about me back home, because I love it here at City and I want to stay.

The pace of the English Premiership suits my game and I'm sure I can be a success here. The fans have been so kind and friendly and Manchester is a great place to be."

The Kippax terrace, which had stood since 1923 and had millions of people stand on its sturdy concrete foundations, was levelled at the end of the 1993/94 season and the bulk of the partisan home support relocated to the North Stand. For a while, the 1994/95 campaign would be a magical, electrically-charged affair with Messrs Rösler, Beagrie and Walsh in superlative form. Niall Quinn had returned to fitness and Nicky Summerbee had arrived from Swindon Town. After having the weakest attack in the Premiership, Horton now had one of the best – an embarrassment of riches that gelled like a dream.

Rösler had become an instant crowd favourite and in the Blues' first two home games of the new campaign he scored three goals as City beat West Ham 3-0 and Everton 4-0. After the victory over the Toffees, commentator Clive Tyldesley asked Uwe how he felt being compared to Tottenham's German sensation Jürgen Klinsmann, who was arguably the hottest striker in the Premiership at that time. He replied: "Yes, but only from the TV."

T-shirts appeared with the message 'Uwe's granddad bombed Old Trafford' as further proof of his popularity became more evident and at Maine Road, when the team seemed inspired whenever they attacked the North Stand, which was an incredible place to be. Loud, constantly singing and inspirational – the Kippax may have been no more than rubble but its spirit lived on.

In truth, this chapter could easily have been about Paul Walsh, Peter Beagrie or Niall Quinn, all of whom were immense crowd favourites. Walsh had a never-say-die attitude the City fans adored. Blessed with an abundance of skill and heart as big as a lion, Walsh had arguably found his spiritual home at Maine Road, and played arguably the best football of his career alongside Rösler, with Beagrie and Summerbee whipping in perfect crosses he was as close to striker-heaven as it's possible to get.

As for Beagrie, he fitted perfectly into the category of Cult Hero in that he was a pure entertainer, easily the best since Rodney Marsh and a fantastic winger that England completely overlooked for the best part of a decade. Beagrie had the ability to beat any defender with his intricate trickery. On his day, like Shane Warne in cricket, he was unplayable. Mesmerising to watch he could whip the perfect cross in from almost any angle and, in truth deserves a chapter of his own.

Niall Quinn is another prime example of a Cult Hero and again, this writer would expect readers to disagree with his non-selection. I wouldn't have a problem with that and if this book allowed 21 chapters, or even has a follow-up, Quinn will be in the next in line. The elegant 6ft 4in forward began a journey of discovery when he signed for Manchester City from Arsenal in 1990 and arrived with the belief he was little more than a useful target man. As time went on, however, he proved that he was a very skilful and intelligent centre forward – perhaps even better on the ground than he was in the air. He became a hugely popular figure at City, forging a fantastic partnership with David White – another Cult Hero candidate who would make a large number of City fans' top 20 lists. Quinn became a talismanic figure for the Blues, scoring goals, creating chances and, on one occasion, even saving a penalty! Deputising for Tony Coton, who had been shown a red card, he put on the green jersey and faced Derby County's Dean Saunders, but Quinn saved his spot-kick and City went on to win 2-1 – it doesn't get much better than that, does it? That was the day his status as club legend was probably cemented and it's because he breached the longevity levels of fandom that he has been left out of this book.

City continued to enthral the Maine Road fans with their home form during 94/95 with the first nine games yielding six wins and three draws and, more importantly 27 goals scored and just 10 conceded – Rösler had grabbed just four of them, but had played his part to the full. Another five before Christmas meant he'd accumulated nine goals, three less than Walsh but one more than Quinn. The attacking, entertaining style played by Horton's side was food and drink to the City fans – what a pity, then, that only 21,000 were permitted to watch the side at home due to the construction of a new, three-tier Kippax Street stand.

Stefan Karl, another German player had been and gone by this time but another was about to arrive during the second half of the season in the form of midfielder Maurizio Gaudino. The maverick former German international arrived with the reputation of something of a playboy and had been linked to a car theft ring back in his homeland, but nobody doubted his ability as a footballer and he soon had the City fans eating out of the palm of his hand with a series of virtuoso midfield displays. Skilful and intelligent, his curly black hair and swarthy looks gave him the look of a Mexican bandit, and he too, is a good shout for a Cult Hero, with only the brevity of his loan spell working against him.

Rösler, meanwhile, was appreciative of his position as crowd favourite and said at the time of his popularity: "It's a very special relationship and one that means a great deal to me. It never happened to me at any of the clubs I played for in Germany. I am still not accustomed to it and I hope I never will be. When I hear the City fans chanting my name it sends a shiver down my spine. I'd heard a lot about Manchester City before I arrived – and it's turned out to be everything I hoped it would be – and more."

City had lost some of their sparkle as they entered 1995 and the goals were beginning to dry up. Rösler shot to the top of the scoring charts during an FA Cup third round replay against Notts County at Maine Road when his virtuoso performance saw him bag four goals in a 5-2 victory. Meanwhile, Quinn and Walsh's goals dried up, Uwe added another eight goals before the end of the season, taking his tally to 21 for his first full season – a terrific return. And there was even better to come as he won the coveted supporters' Player of the Year award for 1995.

The fans loved his passion, the way he celebrated and remonstrated if he thought he'd been hard done to – it's hard to put a finger on why he was quite as popular as he was, but the constant chanting of his name from the City fans suggested he could do little wrong. The man who brought him to the club, however, was sacked at the end of the 94/95 season and over the summer, Alan Ball would be appointed, and the relationship between the two men would prove to be strained at best.

Ball's start to life as Blues' boss was nothing short of disastrous and the one shining light in his side was new signing Georgi Kinkladze, who is featured elsewhere in this book. Rösler had scored a goal during the final match in front of the old Kippax so it was only right that he should score the first in front of the officially opened New Kippax during the opening day 1-1 draw with Spurs. He scored again in the 2-1 loss at Coventry City four days later and that was enough to keep him top scorer until early October as the Blues failed to score in seven of their next eight games. A 4-0 win against Wycombe meant two more goals for Uwe, but four more blanks left City rock bottom with an unenviable record of failing to score in 10 or their 14 games that season. Uwe decided to ditch his boots following a 6-0 defeat at Anfield, but feelings were running so high that this was misinterpreted as an act of frustration by the angry travelling fans who had sung: "We'll score again, don't know where, don't know when..."

Rösler said after the incident: "I wouldn't upset our supporters for the world. I threw my boots into the crowd at Anfield because I thought one of our fans might make better use of them. I certainly don't want to see those boots again – I'm sick of them. I have worn them for the last four games and I haven't scored a single goal. I wouldn't jeopardise my relationship with our fans."

He meant it too. Since being a small boy, he'd dreamed of such adulation. City, however, were on a downward spiral and the Ball/Rösler relationship was about to explode. He was still second top scorer as the Blues entered the final stretch of the season, Georgian striker Mikhail Kavlashvilli effectively took Uwe's place in the side,

Rösler was furious. His track record was excellent and if Ball thought he could make him the scapegoat, he was wrong. Losing 2-1 to Manchester United at Maine Road, Rösler came on with around 20 minutes to go and soon scored a spectacular equaliser to send Maine Road wild. As described at the beginning of this chapter, Rösler made his anger very public with an emotional celebration that pointed the finger squarely at Alan Ball. The City fans were with him all the way.

The Blues still had time to save themselves and despite losing the derby 3-2 and the next game 3-0 at Wimbledon, Rösler scored the winner in a 1-0 win over Sheffield Wednesday and another 1-0 win at Aston Villa meant a final day win over Liverpool might well save City from the drop.

Trailing 2-0, Rösler pulled a goal back from the spot but despite a 2-2 draw, City were relegated. Kinkladze and Rösler were obvious targets for Premiership clubs but both pledged their future with the club, certain they would be back the following year. Three games into the 1996/97 Division One campaign, Ball was sacked and a succession of managers took on the reins at Maine Road and by Christmas, the Blues were mid-table and had managed just six goals. His relationship with Kinky was fairly productive and he added another 11 goals in the second half of the campaign to finish comfortably as the top scorer for the second successive season.

There was, however, more misery ahead as City again struggled with the demands of the division and despite the likes of Kinkladze and Rösler in the team, they were destined for the as yet uncharted depths of Division Two. Uwe's goals dried up and he would manage just six all season, though he didn't play in every game and in March 1998, he was effectively replaced by new manager Joe Royle, who signed Shaun Goater to lead the line. The pair would play briefly alongside each other, almost as a symbolic gesture of Rösler handing the Cult Hero mantle over to Goater and he made his final appearance for City from the bench during a 1-0 defeat at Middlesbrough. A couple of games later and City were relegated. Goater and another kind of Cult Hero, Paul Dickov, would go on to win the hearts of the City fans while Rösler headed home to Germany to play for Champions League outfit Kaiserslautern.

"I am sad that I cannot say goodbye to the supporters on the pitch," said an emotional Rösler shortly before he left. "I feel part of this football club and always will do, but the manager has said I should go now and I feel disappointed about that. I'm not angry with Joe Royle, but I didn't want everything to end like this.

"The supporters have been fantastic with me, despite all the difficulties over the past two or three years. Of course I will miss them, but I will coming back to see how everyone is getting on. I have made friends in Manchester for life and nobody can take that away from me. My feelings have never changed from the moment I arrived in Manchester – I love City and I love the supporters."

There had been good times – his perfectly-judged lob in the FA Cup fifth round tie at Old Trafford, and there had been bad times, such as the occasions he clashed with City fans at Wycombe and after a morale-sapping home loss to Bury, but Rösler's highs far outweighed his lows. He wanted to keep the bond with the supporters and he was as good as his word when the Blues reached the 1999 play-off final against Gillingham and Uwe drank beer and mixed with the City fans on what would ultimately be a fantastic occasion. His career never quite caught fire the way it had at Maine Road and after Kaiserslautern he had unsuccessful spells with West Bromwich Albion and Southampton before moving to Norway's Lillestrom. His return as a Southampton player resulted in a fantastic reception that reduced the former East German international to tears.

Then, the devastating news that Uwe had cancer spread around Manchester in April 2003 and fans sent hundreds of gifts and cards as the former Blues' star underwent treatment for a tumour in his chest and he was overwhelmed by the reaction from the City fans.

He missed the legends' parade at the final game ever to be played at Maine Road as he continued his recovery and at a meal to mark Shaun Goater's last game for City, a friend of Uwe's called him and the packed restaurant – all Blues – chanted the songs he'd become accustomed to as a player. More than 1,000 messages, cards and gifts inspired him to make a full recovery from the life-threatening condition, and he claimed it was the support of the fans who clearly still loved him that helped him.

There aren't many strikers in this book and certainly no typical English centre-forwards. How typical, then, that a German forward should be among the most popular players of the modern era. His subsequent visits back to the City of Manchester Stadium have resulted in standing ovations. His ambition, he says, is to one day manage Manchester City and as he continued to do well in management - in early 2007 he was the boss at Viking F.K in Norway - who would bet against it?

Top scorer for three out of his four seasons at Maine Road, he performed while many others fell by the wayside. Passionate and whole-hearted – Rösler's time at City will be fondly remembered by those who were lucky enough to witness it.

Georgi Kinkladze

1995-1998: 120 games, 21 goals

FRANCIS LEE HAD taken over as City chairman following an aggressive supporters-led campaign to oust Peter Swales and at last the club could look forward to prosperous times again, with the Sixties legend at the controls and bottomless pockets to finance team rebuilding.

Or so we thought.

The truth was very different and after the popular Brian Horton had been sacked, the Blues' fans waited for the big-name manager who would guide them towards the silverware they craved. George Graham was courted, but his interest in the job appeared to be no more than a touch of flirting, a warning to his present club Leeds United that he'd be off if any club so much as flashed their eyes at him – if he wasn't getting what he demanded at home.

Time moved on and on the eve of the 1995/96 season, the Blues were still managerless. Meanwhile, Lee had dispatched Colin Bell and Tony Book to scout on a little-known Georgian who was playing against Wales at the Millennium Stadium. They returned having seen the midfielder dominate the match and score from 25 yards with an audacious chip that left Neville Southall grasping at the night air. For a sublime winner. Bell and Book's advice to the chairman was simple: sign him up without delay. Lee had seen enough grainy videotape to know that this player was the real deal and with no manager installed, Lee picked up the phone and set the wheels in motion himself. It would be his best decision during his turbulent reign as chairman of Manchester City.

THE MID-NINETIES was a time of 'sexy football' as it was labelled. Swaggering, handsome foreign stars who played the game with style and attitude. David Ginola, Ruud Gullit, Eric Cantona and Juninho – the Premiership was awash with talented imports. City had Uwe Rösler and, briefly, Maurizio Gaudino. There'd been popular players from abroad over the years, but none of them had really gone on to the next level and performed consistently well over a period of time – well nobody since Bert Trautmann, of course. City needed an icon, a player so good that he would leave the fans drooling for more.

The club were in the process of cashing in on the fact the hottest band in the world back in 1995, *Oasis*, were City supporters and the Blues' stock among the fashion-conscious youth soared. If only the team could match the lofty heights set by Burnage's finest. The club needed a Liam Gallagher on the pitch, a charismatic figure prepared to stick two fingers up at the rulebook and do his own thing.

News filtered through of an impending deal for a player whose name was hard to pronounce and nigh on impossible to spell. In all honesty, nobody paid too much attention at all. The Blues had signed their fair share of duck eggs over the years and a fair few of them had arrived from Europe in more recent times so why should things change now? Lee and club secretary Bernard Halford worked feverishly to secure Georgi Kinkladze's signature, fighting off overtures from AC Milan, whose scouts had labelled him as the 'Rivera of the Black Sea'- and a very interested Barcelona and a fee of £2m was agreed with Georgian club Dinamo Tbilisi.

Then Lee announced the news. Alan Ball was to be the new manager of Manchester City. Had the half million supporters of the club (according to a nation-wide poll) been massed in one colossal room, you could have still heard a pin drop. This was not the man some of the loyalest fans in the land wanted to lead their club. Aside from his playing days and a few steady years on the south coast, Ball had achieved very little in management and the fact that he was an old friend of the chairman and was perhaps the only man available – he wasn't the outstanding candidate and wasn't even in the top 50 of most fans' wish lists. The choice smacked of desperation - in fact, the rumour that had been doing the rounds was that Lee had considered taking on the role himself. Within 13 months, he probably wished he had.

Ball was unveiled at the same press conference as Kinkladze, and the media circus paid the quietly-spoken Georgian little attention – all their Christmases had come at once and it seemed everybody save for the chairman and manager could foresee the dark days ahead. Kinky would remain something of a mystery to the dumbstruck support until the opening day of the season.

What they might have learned, had there been better research by the media and, it has to be said, if the Internet been anywhere near as huge as it is today, was that Kinkladze was an incredibly gifted footballer. The 21-year-old playmaker had been a sensation with Tbilisi. He was something of a child genius when it came to football, and his father invested many hours each day towards helping his son make it to the top.

In an area torn by war and poverty, he found money to mix a daily cocktail of fruit juices and vitamins to help his development. His disciplined methods also included making his son take a ball from the bottom of their apartment block's stairs up several flights to their home, without picking it up. He also instructed his son to 'walk' around the apartment on his knees in order to strengthen his legs. But it was while his father was working away that perhaps the most influential coaching came into play, with his mother taking him to Georgian dance classes to perform the traditional dance the *mtiulur* - not a million miles away from ballet. In later years, the balance and grace acquired during this period would materialise itself in the form of graceful dribbling, feigns and a sleight of foot that had to be seen to be believed.

As a boy, Georgi was accepted into Dinamo Tbilisi's academy of excellence aged just 8-years-old and kids and parents would queue up to see him showboat with a ball during training.

During his teenage years, Kinkladze had been loaned out to German club Saarbrucken, but there was animosity from some German players towards players from the Eastern Bloc and he found himself on the end of some over-physical attention when he did play. He stayed briefly with Argentinean side Boca Juniors (spiritual home of his hero Diego Maradona) and even trained with Real Madrid for a time alongside the likes of Raul. His return to the dangerous, mafia-controlled streets of Tbilisi meant that if any serious offer came in, it would be accepted without question, and the same applied for any talented young star at the club who would be safer elsewhere. In fact he was offered to Atletico Madrid for just £200,000, but the Spaniards passed on the deal. Georgian players had been murdered, threatened and kidnapped, officials had been slain in their homeland, torn apart by corruption and gangland violence – it was no place for a precocious young talent to learn their trade and fortunately, Georgi didn't stick around long enough to become another statistic.

In Manchester City, he'd joined a club that, while not winning trophies or playing in European competition, had plenty of potential and a huge fanbase. The squad included Keith Curle, Ian Brightwell, Steve Lomas, Garry Flitcroft, Niall Quinn and Uwe Rosler – enough quality to challenge for Europe, if perhaps three top names were added. Peter Beagrie was injured and fans' favourite Paul Walsh was looking forward to another prosperous season – until Ball inexplicably exchanged him for Portsmouth striker Gerry Creaney. It was a portend of things to come.

Meanwhile, the dust settled on Ball's appointment and he confidently predicted prior to Kinkladze's debut that he would have fans "hanging off the rafters" trying to watch him play and, on this occasion, he was right.

"The rest of England won't be familiar with Kinkladze's name right now," said Ball at the time. "But just you wait until the season starts. Every soccer fan in the country will be talking about him."

CITY OPENED THEIR Premiership campaign with a home game against Tottenham Hotspur and the capacity crowd settled into their seats and enjoyed the warm August sunshine.

Kinkladze, who everyone had by now learned was fortunately nicknamed 'Kinky' in his homeland, played a few neat passes and was generally tidy without taking too many risks in the early exchanges, until a ball came towards him at speed and he nonchalantly stuck out his left foot, and made a deft flick to a team-mate. The crowd roared their approval. It had been an innocuous enough piece of skill, but it was the manner he did it - you could just see this was somebody who found moves such as that incredibly easy. It was natural to him, and as the game wore on, his confidence grew and by the end of the game, which finished 1-1, there was only one man's name on the 30,000 crowd's lips.

City, however, embarked on a soul-destroying run that left them rooted to the bottom of the table without a win in twelve games. Kinky was still adjusting to the pace of English football and apart from some eye-catching dribbles and clever passing, it seemed as though it might not happen for him in England.

The pace of the game was sometimes too hectic and the tactics of the team confusing. Sometimes it would be the long-ball game targeting Quinn, other times Kinky would try things and lay balls into space expecting a team-mate to have read his intentions, only to see the pass harmlessly roll out of play.

Fortunately, by November, the Blues finally found some form and it was no coincidence that Kinky had also found his. Three wins out of four saw the ridiculed Ball pick up the Manager of the Month award and Kinky picked up his first goal, collecting the ball with a minute left on the clock against Aston Villa, then driving towards the box before laying it off for Quinn, who played the one-two perfectly allowing Kinky to slot the ball home.

If there had been any doubters, they were won over in that magical minute of skill and vision. In fact, it would soon become clear that Kinky only scored spectacular goals. His form was imperious – true he could be quiet away from home and at times be ineffective and had not so much as a defensive bone in his body – he didn't 'do' tackles, either. But when he turned on the style, he could win a match single-handedly and there are only a handful of players in the world who can do that whenever the mood takes them. The team were still in a precarious position, but the love affair with Kinkladze had begun in earnest although a succession of expensive flops joined the club – Michael Frontzeck and Nigel Clough among them.

In a terribly timed bid to swell club coffers, the influential Garry Flitcroft was sold to Blackburn for £3.5m as the relegation haunted Blues entered the run-in. Ball seemed helpless to halt the slide towards the First Division and only Kinky lightened the dark days of the 1995/96 season with the odd match-winning display. Yet he looked frustrated, clever passes were continually misjudged by team-mates, incisive runs forward were wasted and the general feel was that the majority of the team just weren't on the same wavelength. If there was one defining moment in his City career, it was the home game with Southampton in March 1996. With the scores level at 0-0, Kinky picked up the ball on the right and moved with purpose towards goal. He skipped past a couple of challenges, shimmied between the centre backs and was, all of a sudden, one-on-one with the Southampton keeper Dave Beasant. He approached goal, feigned to shoot, flooring Beasant before gently lifting the ball over him and into the back of the net. It was a moment of pure genius and Maine Road went crazy. The goal was beamed around the world and it seemed that the Premiership's best-kept secret was over.

Ironically, a players' strike in Italy meant there were no Serie A games that weekend and the Premiership instead took centre stage. One goal in particular would be replayed over and over... It was just a matter of time before Juventus or AC Milan made their moves, the press informed us. Celtic and Liverpool were reportedly lining up £10m bids, too as City limped towards the last game of the season, knowing that a win over Liverpool would probably be enough to keep them afloat.

Kinky gave his all, as did the whole team, but at 2-0 down, it looked hopeless. The Georgian came out after the break looking determined to try and rescue the situation himself, and soon won a penalty, but though the game ended 2-2, all the other teams on the same points total but with better goal differences, also picked up a point. Kinky left the pitch in tears and that, everyone thought, was that.

But the Georgian people have a reputation for loyalty and, after lengthy talks at the chairman's Cheshire mansion, Lee convinced the player he freely admitted he thought of as a son, to spearhead a return to the Premiership. Quite why such a talent, at the top of his game and with a host of top British and European sides desperate to sign him, would choose life in Division One was something of a mystery, but save to say the bond between player and fans became watertight. This was loyalty above and beyond the call of duty and in an age when mercenary footballers were commonplace and whereever they lay their lucrative contract, that was their home, Kinkladze stayed to fight the cause. It was unheard of.

WITHIN THREE GAMES of the start of the 1996/97 season, Ball was sacked and a succession of managers would preside over the club, none of whom seemed to know how best to utilise the magnificent talent in their midst, before Frank Clark took over on a lengthy deal. Kinky's talent shone through like a beacon and it was at times embarrassing that he was so much better than the other dross on show. He scored wonderful goals, made many others while all the time being hacked and bullied by journeymen defenders and midfielders determined to stop the Georgian by any means necessary. It was all too transparent that if you stopped Kinky, you stopped City and took something from the game. Opposition managers employed hatchet men to scythe down the Blues' No.10 or hit him so hard with borderline legal tackles, that he sometimes didn't get up.

Yet he didn't hide and the fans loved him for it. He seemed to enjoy life in Manchester and was seen in the company of rock stars such as Noel Gallagher and he even bought a £100,000 Ferrari – though he was lucky to escape with his life when a race with team-mate Nicky Summerbee ended in an horrific crash into a motorway bridge. Kinkladze escaped with a few cuts and bruises but the car was a complete write-off – shaken, but not stirred, he was back in the starting line-up with a few days.

It was impossible to compare him to any midfielder of the past because he was unique. He couldn't do what Colin Bell did, but then even the majestic Bell wasn't capable of the individual skill Kinkladze possessed – only Ronaldinho and Diego Maradona spring to mind ability-wise – and that's no exaggeration. Rodney Marsh was probably the closest in terms of individual brilliance, but even he wasn't in the same league, plus Kinky was more of a team player.

The general opinion was that this was City's most gifted player ever, playing in one of the worst teams for four decades. A mid-table finish was guaranteed by the time the Blues took on Reading for the final match of the season. Kinky was injured, but the City fans, realising that this would probably be the last time to say thanks for the memories, organised Georgi Kinkladze Day.

Flags, electronic messages, songs and placards written in Georgian – the City fans pulled out every stop to try and keep the only reason most of them still felt like watching the team from leaving. It was heartfelt, moving and for the injured idol watching from the stands, almost too much to take.

City rallied from 2-0 down to beat Reading 3-2 and when the final whistle blew, nobody left. The players walked back out for a 'lap of honour' but it wasn't until a beige-suited Kinky was led, a little sheepishly, to the centre circle, that the 28,000 crowd rose as one. He received a standing ovation as he walked around the ground and, for many, it seemed as though he was saying goodbye.

There also seemed a dejection among the rest of the team that they were seemingly thought so little of, but the outpouring of affection towards a player who had shelved his own ambitions in order to try and help City back to the top division again, was greatly appreciated and this was a heartfelt 'thanks'.

As dozens of supporters hung around his Wilmslow home, Georgi remarked to a family member, 'How can I leave here when there is so much love?' It was indeed a love story, but like the greatest tales of that genre, it was tinged with tragedy, at least in a football sense.

Incredibly, Lee again convinced Kinkladze to give it one last try. It was almost cruel. Interest in his signature had cooled and as he began his third season at Maine Road, he'd become little more than a dancing bear, performing when he had to in the knowledge that the chains were binding. True, he loved the fans but it was clear in his body language that he wanted to be elsewhere.

The physical toll of leaving the pitch each week battered and bruised coupled with the mental anguish and ineffectiveness of his team-mates and defeats at the hands of clubs like Lincoln City left a pale shadow of the twinkle-toed genius that had made fools of some of the best defenders in the world just two years earlier.

When Joe Royle was appointed the new manager in early 1998, he immediately expressed concern over what he believed was 'an unhealthy obsession' with Kinkladze.

He made it clear that the player would be available at the right price and opted to drop him for several games. In a pivotal clash away to Port Vale, Royle pitched Kinky into the mix, almost certainly to prove to even his most ardent of admirers that the muddy pitches and dogs of war attitude needed to survive meant there was no room for a talent such as his. Virtually anonymous, Kinky was substituted while City fans argued amongst themselves. The love affair apparently over, a £5.5m deal was struck with Ajax.

He wouldn't join the Dutch giants until the end of the season and made it clear he was up for the fight if needed – in fact, he implored Royle to play him in the run-in because he genuinely believed he could help City avoid the unthinkable – the drop to the nation's third tier, then known as Division Two for the first time in the club's proud 111-year history. Him not being in the team had not altered the poor form, so making him the scapegoat slightly misfired.

With time running out and only a handful of games remaining, Royle succumbed to fan pressure and picked Kinky to play against QPR. When a free kick was awarded half a minute into the game, Kinky placed it to his liking, ran up and curled a 30-yard drive past the keeper and stood fairly motionless as he was mobbed by team-mates.

Lacking match fitness, he soon tired and the 2-2 draw did little to enhance survival hopes. When selected for Georgia's friendly in Tunisia, Kinky was effectively ruled out of the final day decider at Stoke. The Blues, marooned third from the bottom needed any of the three sides above them to drop points while winning themselves in order to stay up.

Because the final day's games were due to be played on a Sunday, Kinky could still make it back to play, as Georgia were in action 24 hours earlier. A private jet was organised by the club to bring the player back and he was named as a substitute for the visit to the Britannia Stadium – he knew this was his final farewell and he didn't want to miss it at any cost.

City led 4-2 when Shaun Goater injured his shoulder and Georgi Kinkladze came on to a hero's welcome from the 8,000 travelling City fans. Other latest scores meant that the supporters knew victory was almost certainly futile and when the final whistle blew, all the travelling thousands wanted to do was pay homage to Kinkladze. He walked towards them in tears and flung his boots into the crowd before disappearing down the tunnel for the last time.

ROYLE COULD NOW continue his team rebuilding without distraction and, more importantly, with a healthy kitty to dip into. Kinky began life as an Ajax player and periodically, groups of City fans would make the pilgrimage to Amsterdam to see their hero.

The Dutch coach didn't play his record buy to his strengths and played him out of position on the left wing. Kinkladze had been bought to replace Ajax legend Jari Litmanen who had seemed to be Barcelona-bound, but the deal fell through at a late stage and he remained in Amsterdam. Litmanen would retain his central midfield role and Kinky's future was effectively doomed to fail and he played just a dozen games before losing his place completely. The fans didn't take to him and thought of him as a huge waste of money and after a couple of miserable years, he returned to England with Derby County after manager Jim, Smith called Franny Lee to ask if he was worth the gamble. Lee told him it wasn't a gamble and after initially joining the Rams on loan, he joined on a permanent deal for £3.5m.

He showed occasional flashes of brilliance at Pride Park and was a huge crowd favourite. He was welcomed like a long, lost son on his return to Maine Road – though he was a Derby player and received standing ovations as he ran over to take corners and, for a time, it was like the old days. He later was forced to beg, steal or borrow in order to try and find a club that would take him on, trialing for Portsmouth, Leeds and Bolton before heading off to Cyprus to play Anorthosis Famagusta with his old Georgia team-mate Temuri Ketsbaia. At the time of writing, he was making something of a comeback with Russian outfit FC Rubin Kazan.

Kinky was a hero to thousands because he stayed and ultimately sacrificed his own career to serve Manchester City. He took the punishment on the pitch from opponents and, for a time, lifted everyone a little higher. He was always capable of something special and, he could be a spectator for 89 minutes then go and win the game with a magical piece of skill. He was, without doubt, the greatest talent ever to play for City, but history tells us that he was also part of one of, statistically at least, the worst teams on record. Even today, debate rages as to how good Kinky really was for Manchester City – was he a luxurious distraction or was he a world great, imprisoned by mediocrity? Most probably, it was just a case of bad timing - he was the right player at the wrong time. Such is the very essence of the Cult Hero.

Andy Morrison

1998-2001: 39 games, 4 goals

GEORGI KINKLADZE PICKED the ball up for City around the centre circle and took on a lumbering Huddersfield Town defender on the halfway line at Maine Road. Kinky shimmied one way, then the next before pushing the ball through the hapless marker's legs, much to the delight of the home fans – it was a cruel mismatch, but it wasn't quite over on this occasion. As the little Georgian pushed the ball forward and away from the beefy No.5 with a blond crew-cut and the build of a military drill sergeant and looked ahead for a killer through ball, the tortured Huddersfield centre-half almost cut Kinkladze in half with a desperate tackle, part frustration, part rage but all in the name of retribution. The City fans roared their disapproval and the inevitable "You fat bastard! You fat bastard!" echoed around the old stadium with all fingers pointing at the perpetuator. A yellow card was brandished and the referee noted the name of Andy Morrison. Within a year, Morrison would be doing the same kind of thing in a Manchester City shirt. And the fans worshipped him for it.

JOE ROYLE'S WORST nightmare was coming true. City's pre-season promotion favourites tag looked like a bad joke as a succession of teams left Maine Road with some kind of reward for their efforts. Wrexham, Chesterfield, Burnley, Preston and Reading all took a point or more while Lincoln beat the Blues 2-1 at Sincil Bank to further deepen the depression surrounding the comatose giant. There wasn't much money available and his options were severely limited. One of the reasons City were doing so badly was that they could be bullied on the pitch by the gnarly streetwise forwards that had earned their living the hard way and an afternoon giving a naive ex-Premiership defender a hard time for 90 minutes was too good an opportunity to pass up. Lightweights like Nick Fenton (centre-half) and Gary Mason (midfield) were all too easy to outmuscle and there seemed little leadership within the team.

Royle needed a warrior, a captain fantastic prepared to go to war and inspire the troops, somebody who would sweat blood for the shirt. A quick phone call to his counterpart Peter Jackson at Huddersfield and a month's loan for Andy Morrison was secured. The Inverness-born central defender with a West Country accent had wandered around the lower leagues starting his career with Plymouth Argyle. Blackburn Rovers would later pay £500,000 for his services, and he was a member of the squad when they won the Premiership in 1993, though little more than a bit-part player at best, playing just five times for the Ewood Park side. He was soon on the move again, joining Blackpool for £250,000 but did sufficiently well enough for the Seasiders to be sold on for twice that fee when former City boss Brian Horton took him to Huddersfield where he soon became a firm favourite among the Terriers' fans. Andy was made captain and played an influential role as the West Yorkshire side chased promotion to the Premiership. Morrison's contract was up by the time Peter Jackson took over as manager and the pair clashed several times before it became clear that the town wasn't big enough for the both of them.

Joe Royle reckoned Morrison might just be the right kind of character to drag his misfiring team up the table – if not out of respect then out of raw fear.

Morrison cut an ominous figure. Think heavyweight boxer mixed with nightclub bouncer. He had well-documented off-field problems including anger management issues, but Royle had no hesitation in signing the player or in naming him to play in the team that faced Colchester United at Maine Road on a most appropriate date - Hallowe'en 1998.

It nearly turned into another horror show as the plucky visitors looked set to leave with a 1-1 draw, but Morrison launched himself at a cross in the last minute and powered home a trademark header to clinch a 2-1 win for the Blues. It was the perfect start and the City fans that had derided Morrison just a year earlier now chanted his name as they left the ground. It could be argued that Morrison's explosive start to his City career was the reason he would become such a cult figure amongst the supporters – it certainly played a part, but, as with many Manchester City Cult Heroes, it was the passion shown while wearing the sky blue jersey that endeared him the most to the fans – they just can't stomach somebody who puts their all into each performance and opts out of 50-50 balls, however many fancy flicks and neat passes they make. Passion, commitment and courage – that's all they ask for. If a player gives them what they demand, their backing is total.

Nonetheless, Morrison was quick to show that he had other strings to his bow and during his second game for the Blues he scored a quite spectacular goal that cemented his popularity of the 6,000 travelling fans –lurking on the edge of the Oldham Athletic box the ball fell to Morrison 20 yards out and he hit as sweet a volley into the roof of the net as you are ever likely to see. The cocky celebration – cheeks puffed out and chest strutting out like a proud cockerel, he took all the plaudits and why not? This was probably the first time he'd had such adulation and he was determined to enjoy it. The sudden upturn in fortunes for the

Blues – the 3-0 win at Boundary Park was easily the best display of the season was evidence enough that Mozzer was going to be the talisman that rescued the club from obscurity. Chants of 'Sign him up!' rang round Maine Road in the next game and Royle wasted no time in making the loan deal a permanent one, paying just £80,000 to Huddersfield for his services.

It wouldn't be all plain sailing, though, and there would be no league wins in the next four league games and Morrison was absent from the team that then lost 2-1 at York City that saw the Blues slump to their lowest league position in 118 years of existence. It was to be a pivotal moment and City would only climb upwards and onwards from that moment on and at the forefront of the charge was Andy Morrison who was determined not to let down the manager who had given him his big chance or the legion of supporters who adopted him as their new idol.

Royle made 'Mozzer' the new skipper and it soon became clear that he was much more than an imposing physical presence on the pitch. He was an excellent passer and had good technique – skills that often belied his shape and size, but he was capable of placing a 50-yard pass on a sixpence, so to speak.

In the great tradition of war-horses like Mike Doyle and Gerry Gow, however, Morrison was as tough as old boots and his occasional clashes with the hard men of his era invariably came under the spotlight. During one particularly bruising battle at Selhurst Park, City took on Wimbledon in an FA Cup third round tie, Mozzer clashed with Carl Cort and the pair endured a brutal battle and though the Dons edged the match 1-0, the duel ended about even – and in an early bath for both players.

City's skipper wouldn't accept anything but total commitment and players like Paul Dickov, Tony Vaughan, Michael Brown and Jamie Pollock responded – far from City looking like a team of pushovers, during the second half of the campaign, the Blues had the hard edge needed to survive the lower leagues and the types of players who earned their living there. A 12-match unbeaten run was ended by Oldham at Maine Road, but

Morrison's troublesome knee problems occasionally kept him sidelined. How many times he played when injured only Mozzer knows, but he pushed himself to the limits until the Blues were guaranteed a play-off spot – the very least that had been expected at the start of the season, but still an amazing feat considering they'd been in twelfth position a week before Christmas.

In an effort to make a possible play-off final, Mozzer had to rest up for a fortnight while his team-mates took on Wigan Athletic in the play-off semi-final, which they just edged 2-1 on aggregate. His replacement, Tony Vaughan made way for Morrison's return in the play-off final against Gillingham at Wembley, but it was a gamble that would almost backfire on the player and Joe Royle as he limped off in the first half, unable to take any further part.

City very nearly blew their chance of promotion and the dramas against Gillingham are well documented, but with a place in the First Division secured in the most incredible circumstances, Morrison climbed the famous Wembley steps to lift the play-off trophy to the 40,000 ecstatic fans. It was undoubtedly the proudest moment of his career and he had done exactly what Joe Royle had asked him to – lead the club out of the depths of despair by restoring hope and belief – and the Blues were now just one good season away from the Premiership

Royle recognised the value and contribution his skipper had given him and in later years would say: "Big clubs in Division Two are a scalp and everyone wants to beat them. City were the biggest show in town and everyone wanted to see us. They'd welcome us, turn up in their thousands and then try and kick us off the pitch. It was hard for us, but we got the hang of it. The catalyst for us was signing Andy Morrison – he was the man for us and the man for the division. He dragged us up kicking and screaming. We only got him because of his injury record and because he'd had a major fall-out with the manager at Huddersfield. He was as strong as they come and feared nobody – he played a big part in turning things round for us."

Ian Bishop claimed that Morrison's influence at Maine Road "could not be overstated," but the crippling knee problems that had dogged his career were about to resurface with a vengeance and just how great the cost was to a player who played when he shouldn't have is unclear, but his determination to see the job through would now take its toll – and cost him a chance to play for his country.

Though regarded by some as a loose cannon, Mozzer's disciplinary record at City wasn't actually too bad, but it was set to worsen and he was sent off for licking Stan Collymore's nose and mouth during a stormy clash at Fulham! He later claimed that he didn't know why he did it but if he hadn't, he would have given Collymore "a slap" - so it was the lesser of two evils in his book!

Disciplinary problems or not, Scotland boss Craig Brown was believed to be on the verge of calling the Inverness-born defender (with a West Country accent) into his team for the first time for the crucial Euro 2000 qualifier against England, in October 1999. Cruelly, a knee injury sustained at Port Vale finished Mozzer's season and kept him out of the Blues' meteoric rise back to the Premiership and his chance of representing his country would never present itself again. It seemed he was fated to inspire those around him to loftier heights but reap little in the way of rewards himself.

Forced to watch his team-mates sweep all aside from the stands, he once said: "I was watching us live away to Charlton, but with 15 minutes left, I gave up. I put on *Teletext* instead. Even then I covered half the screen and knew that if the Charlton score remained nil, we'd won."

The fans loved that he was, in their eyes, one of their own. There were no airs or graces about him – what you saw is what you got. You could have a pint with Andy Morrison and enjoy the craic with him – so the supporters imagined. He was a man's man and when it came to captains of Manchester City, he was up there with the likes of Doyle and Paul – very much from the no-nonsense old school of defending.

Following a knee operation, it would be 14 months before he was fit enough to play for the Blues again and Royle had been forced to reinforce his back four with the high-profile purchases of Spencer Prior from Derby County, Steve Howey from Newcastle United and the highly-rated Republic of Ireland international Richard Dunne from Everton.

Desperate to save his City career, he spent loan spells at Blackpool and Crystal Palace in a bid to regain full fitness and, finally, in December 2000 he played in a League Cup-tie against Ipswich, receiving a hero's welcome from the City fans. He turned in a man-of-the-match performance and could at last represent City in the Premiership and his first game for the Blues at that level again saw him voted as the best player on the pitch.

He delighted the City supporters again by scoring a bullet header from a Danny Tiatto corner in a FA Cup tie against Birmingham City in January 2001 – typical Roy of the Rovers stuff that capped a magnificent comeback match. Sadly, this was to be his last goal for the club. He would make his final appearance in a 4-2 FA Cup defeat at Liverpool and was cautioned by police for squirting water at Liverpool fans as he was substituted.

He couldn't force his way back into the side and the Blues' boss was prepared to let the player move on, though Morrison wasn't prepared to leave without a fight. Despite a deal with Bristol City being agreed in March 2001, Morrison wanted to stay with the club he loved and the fans that loved him for what he was and represented. Duty-bound, he travelled down to Ashton Gate for talks but the £150,00 deal collapsed with the burly centre-half unhappy about the situation..

"I went down and spoke to Bristol, but things weren't right, so it's on hold at the moment," he said at the time. "I want to stay and I've made that perfectly clear, but it's been made obvious to me that I'm not wanted. I know where I stand now and it's plainly obvious."

He remained at the club but the Blues were relegated at the end of the season and Joe Royle was sacked and effectively,

Morrison's career at City was over. New manager Kevin Keegan wanted his own men in and Mozzer wasn't what you'd call a typical Keegan player. He was, however, sent out on loan again by the City boss in a bid to again find fitness and match sharpness but it was while he was at Sheffield United that he picked up the knee injury that would effectively end his playing career. The club agreed to pay up the remainder of his contract – about three months – in March 2002 and Keegan paid tribute to the strapping defender saying: "Andy gained cult status when the club gained promotion. He is a first-class professional and deserves a chance to further his career."

Keegan invited Morrison to say a last goodbye prior to the Blues' home game with Crystal Palace and the standing ovation he received as he waved from the centre circle with his two children, Aaron and Brook, clearly moved the former skipper. He said: "It was a special day and a nice to be able to say goodbye to the fans in the way I did.

"I'm not really the type of person that gets emotional over those type of things but it was nice. Kevin Keegan suggested the idea for me to say goodbye properly and I jumped at the chance. We came to an amicable agreement given that my contract was up in June and now I can concentrate on getting completely fit again."

However, despite his optimism, a couple of attempts to return to playing were aborted when it became clear that he physically could not play again and he later moved into management as a coach at Worcester City.

Reflecting on his career and why it never reached the heights it perhaps should have done, Morrison said: "I am a firm believer that things happen for a reason. There is no doubt that my career could have gone a different way, but it didn't and I am just grateful that I had my time with City, it was a fantastic experience.

"My personality has led me to do certain things that I shouldn't have done, but I feel I am in a great position to make sure that others don't fall for the same temptations and get themselves in the same kind of scrapes.

"People have seen the fighter on the pitch, but anyone who has played alongside me or knows me understands that there is a different side to me. I absolutely know the pit-falls. I know what makes a good player and I now what makes a player successful. I know also the other side on how the way you live your life affects your career. I know where it can lead if the commitment is not there. I have had both sides of the coin.

"It has been a rocky road for me but I am determined that the traits in my personality that perhaps held me back as a young player with not stop me from being the best possible coach that I can be.

"There is no doubt that I could have achieved so much more from my career but I believe in fate and that my career went exactly the way it was meant to. Life turns out how it is meant to go and I was very fortunate that towards the end of my playing days I got a move to Manchester City that was perhaps a reward for the hard work I put in towards the latter stages of my career.

"I finally woke up and realised that I needed to make more of my career and the sacrifices and dedication that I made then got me the chance to play for a great club. I know now I should have made those same sacrifices when I was much, much younger but you live and learn and that is something I can pass on to a new generation of players.

"My future is now an open book. It is frightening not knowing what the future holds but it is also exciting because it is a new chapter in my life. I am heading off in a different way. This is real life now. It's not simple sailing any more but I am prepared for it. It's all ifs and buts but my determination is as fierce as ever."

So why does Andy Morrison deserve to be a cult hero and not, say Spencer Prior, Steve Howey or Gerard Wiekens who all enjoyed popularity and reasonable success during their time at City? The answer is Morrison could never give any less than his all, and it was clear in the straining neck muscles evident every time he went up for a header, or the crunching tackles that would often leave opponents winded or worse, or the gesticulations to the crowd after a goal or to gee the team on. Clenched teeth, fists raised with a wry sense of humour thrown in for good measure, Mozzer lived and breathed his role as Manchester City captain and, just for a while, he got his rewards in adulation and respect. He's since moved into coaching and is sure to be a success due to his organisational skills and passion for the game. Skilful and far more intelligent than he was perhaps given credit for, Andy Morrison is the living embodiment of a Cult Hero and was the football equivalent of a mercenary soldier – City's very own warrior of the wastelands. If he had played with war paint on his face, nobody would have been surprised. More to the point, nobody would have told him to wipe it off.

Ali Benarbia

2001-2003: 78 games, 11 goals

CITY FANS LOVE to hark back to the golden era of Bell, Lee and Summerbee, and why not? Some clubs don't have any golden eras to hark back on, so fans should be allowed to reminisce. But one of the reasons those days are still talked of so fondly, is down to the fact the Blues have failed to win a trophy since 1976 and the playing staff has, since the seventies, been largely forgettable. City fans love to have an idol, but it wasn't until Georgi Kinkladze's arrival in 1995 that the supporters had a player to worship and then in 2001, like the proverbial No.42 bus, two come along at once. But out of the two exceptional talents, who did the fans make their cult hero? Ali Benarbia or Eyal Berkovic? Both were brilliant footballers, so why did one edge it over the other…?

THE SUBLIME SKILLS and vision of diminutive Algerian playmaker Ali Benarbia sparked the fuse that lit up City's spectacular domination of Division One during the 2001/02 season. His arrival at Maine Road, in the twilight of a glittering career and aged 32, was the catalyst that put a stuttering promotion campaign from Kevin Keegan's side firmly back on track.

Having lost the mercurial Eyal Berkovic to injury for several weeks following a defeat at Norwich, Keegan began to search for a replacement who could, basically, do what Eyal did – and there weren't too many of them around.

Berkovic had made his debut a few weeks earlier in the 3-0 opening day defeat of Watford – both his and Keegan's first game for City – and the fans took to him immediately. Some players are, in the supporters' eyes, born to play for Manchester City. The fans ask for just two things – a big heart and a touch of flair and if you fall into even just one of those categories, you'll never have to buy a drink in Manchester again.

Ali Benarbia was a gifted player who had spent almost his entire career in France, but he wanted one last hurrah abroad and he'd always fancied a crack at playing in England. Born in Oran, Algeria in 1968, he would spend just three years of his life in his birth country before his family moved to France for a new life, as many Algerians did and still do.

His ability was spotted at an early age and he played as a teenager for FC Martigues from 1987 and he'd remain there until 1995. He then had a succession of moves to different French clubs, starting with Monaco, Bordeaux and finally Paris St Germain. For years Benarbia, by now a French citizen, had harboured hopes of playing international football for France, but a succession of talented French playmakers – among their number Zinedine Zidane – meant he was constantly overlooked and he decided to represent Algeria relatively late in his career. Quite how the French could ignore one of the most consistently excellent midfielders for an entire decade is a complete mystery and it is perhaps the reason he decided to quit the country.

Benarbia's name was circulated among a number of Premiership clubs and he was invited over for a trial with Sunderland, but was disappointed with the way things went. When he was asked to play in a second session because the manager had missed the first and feeling he shouldn't need to prove himself at that stage of his career, he left. He felt he'd achieved enough in the game to be treated with a little more respect than he was during his short time on Wearside and, being very much his own man, he told Peter Reid he was no longer interested in signing for the Black Cats.

Fortunately for City, Benarbia, a free agent, stopped off at Carrington to see Alioune Toure who he knew from his days with Paris St Germain. The pair shared the same agent and Ali met him in the players' canteen and they chatted about old times.

While he was there, Keegan got talking to him and enjoyed a spot of lunch with him. He asked him what he was up to and who he was playing for and when Ali told him he was unattached, Keegan asked if he'd like to take part in the afternoon session with the rest of the squad. It took just a few minutes of Benarbia in action for Keegan to realise he was in the midst of a genius. A skilful, experienced playmaker – and he'd practically fallen into his lap!

The Black Cats' loss soon became City's gain as the player twice voted French Footballer of the Year, made an immediate impression on the club and would soon became an idol to the fans.

The transfer was completed on Friday, 14 September 2001, and was arguably the best piece of business conducted by Keegan as City manager.

On signing for Blues, the Algerian-born, French-raised Benarbia said: "Ever since I was a boy I have dreamed of playing in English football and now I have that opportunity I am going to make the most of it. I grew up watching English football and in particular Liverpool at a time when Kevin Keegan was one of their star players.

"This is the right moment for me to be playing in England and at Manchester City. I know it is a big club and I know we will win promotion to the Premiership at the end of the season."

He was outstanding on his debut, helping destroy Birmingham 3-0 at Maine Road by setting up two of the goals and he received a standing ovation from the 31,000 fans as he left the pitch. He went on to score four times in his first seven appearances.

Chants of "Ali, Ali, Ali!" coupled with bows of devotion from his legion of new admirers became commonplace across the country, in locations that to him must have seemed a million miles away from the Champions League – his former stomping ground.

Benarbia had been a huge crowd favourite but the City fans were more demonstrative than any of the others he'd ever played in front of. He was a football genius and after six years without any midfield creativity, suddenly the City fans had two in Benarbia (or 'Ali B' as he became better known) and Berkovic. It wasn't lost on the City fans that perhaps only their club could house an Arab and a Jew together as a midfield partnership, but it was explosive only in terms of creativity and invention.

But while Eyal was somewhat faint-hearted on certain occasions and would often chicken out of 50-50 challenges, Ali was small in stature, but solid and stocky. He could hold his own and was wily enough to handle some of the punishment dished out in his direction.

Never one to hide when things weren't going well, or like some foreign players, not relish a winter evening away fixture in rainy Rotherham, Benarbia was as whole-hearted and inspirational as fans could wish for. He was also way too good for Division One football. After his debut, Keegan revealed that having encountered Benarbia's destructive skills when his former club Newcastle had met Monaco in the Champions League, he had no qualms about pitching him into action so soon after signing him.

"People in England may not have heard too much about him but Ali is no mug," he said at the time. "He has three French championship medals. One was with Monaco, which is where I, and Arthur Cox in particular, knew him from.

"He is a top-class player, well-known throughout France and what was on view against Birmingham is only the tip of the iceberg."

How prophetic the words of the former England manager would prove to be. Team-mates, it seemed, could not believe their luck to be playing alongside him. A week after his debut, during a 6-2 away win at Sheffield Wednesday, Benarbia was, at times, on a different planet, prompting Paulo Wanchope to remark: "He can see you when you can't even see yourself!" His performance that day was world class, make no mistake, and he destroyed Wednesday with the kind of football usually reserved for players wearing the yellow and blue of Brazil. Shaun Goater claimed that strikers were known to go hiding on certain occasions but said those days were over now Ali had arrived. "No matter where we are, he finds us!" he said.

When Berkovic returned from injury, many reporters asked Keegan who he would select for the playmaker role in his side. Keegan, to his eternal credit, said: "I'm constantly asked which player I will select out of Ali and Eyal – I say, why not play both?" And he did. For all his flaws, Keegan knew good football and he sensed the chemistry of two of Europe's most talented midfielders would carry his side all the way back to the Premiership. It was an electric partnership – as good as anything seen at Maine Road for many a long year.

Shaun Goater, Darren Huckerby, Wanchope and latterly Jon Macken were the beneficiaries of the midfield maestros' artistry. The multi-lingual Benarbia, who had learned his trade under Arsene Wenger at Monaco, was soon hailed as the best City player since Georgi Kinkladze.

But unlike the little Georgian, Benarbia was the heartbeat of a winning team, hungry for success and determined to grab promotion and do it in a style that befitted the precocious talents within the team – something Kinkladze never had the pleasure of. In short, whereas Kinky had players around him that just weren't good enough for most of his time at Maine Road, Benarbia had quality in abundance alongside him and went on to score eight goals in 42 appearances as Keegan's side swept all before them during the promotion season, playing the kind of football many City fans had only dreamed of.

Some of his flicks, dummies and passes were on another plain and for Goater in particular, it was manna from heaven as he became the first City striker in 30 years to top 30 goals in a season. "He was my sat-nav!" said Goater. "Ali could thread a ball through the eye of a needle and once I managed to tune into his wavelength, I knew if I made the run, Ali would find me."

One goal proved Goater's point perfectly. City were away to Gillingham and the ball found its way to Benarbia on the edge of the box. He somehow managed to lift the ball up off the floor with a back-heeled flick towards Goater who volleyed home a sweet shot into the bottom corner. More often than not, when Benarbia made a goal, the players went to him rather than the scorer!

It was an incredible season and though there were several heroes in the team, Benarbia was the orchestra's conductor – and they played beautiful music!

He was a character and would invariably raise a smile during a game, whether it be a piece of skill or an off-the-ball incident. After losing a front tooth in a physically bruising encounter at home to Crystal Palace, he ran after the referee grinning to show the gap where one of his teeth used to be to show he'd had an elbow in the mouth. He then showed the fans in the Kippax and shook his head before carrying on with the game. It endeared him further to the fans, who continued to bow each time he took a corner or throw-in, because he didn't make a fuss and just got on with it.

Berkovic, a bargain £1.5m signing from Celtic, was hugely popular, too, but there was always something suspect about his temperament that didn't quite take him to the next level. He was a fiery character, very expressive and at times dramatic but was capable of individual brilliance as well as being a superb team player. He made a magnificent start to his Maine Road career by scoring one and creating another in a 3-0 win over Watford. His one flaw, in the eyes of the supporters, was his fear of getting hurt and it caused him to pull out of numerous challenges. It wasn't that the fans thought he should be clattering opponents and winning the ball – the City fans are as knowledgeable as any set of supporters, but when they see one of their players skip over a tackle and lose the ball, they will let him know they don't approve.

It's a pity, because Berkovic was an exceptional talent and the manner of his departure from City was handled poorly by Keegan, who fell out with the Israeli over a contract extension. Basically, Eyal wanted the club to commit to a deal that would extend his stay with the club a further two years and somewhere down the line it became a problem, god knows why, and would eventually end with the player moving to Portsmouth for peanuts.

Berkovic also once ran his finger across his throat to a City fan he somehow got in an argument with during a League Cup tie with Crewe. Whatever had been said, it was a stupid thing to do and again raised doubts about his temperament. For those reasons alone, Ali would have to edge the cult hero honours.

Danny Tiatto, another firebrand midfielder was a hugely popular figure at City. He'd been with the club several years and his game was based on total commitment and all-out aggression. He didn't score goals and rarely made them, but he could produce a crunching tackle that could lift the whole team and supporters and he was prepared to get hurt in the name of Manchester City. Tiatto's endeavour was also his flaw, and he was sent off so many times that there was a question mark as to whether a pumped-up Tiatto was an asset or a liability. As with Berkovic, the deficiencies in Tiatto's game would make Ali more of a cult hero, even if both the other challengers for the title were hugely popular.

After Stuart Pearce retired from playing in favour of a move into coaching, Keegan named Benarbia as the new team captain. His appointment was universally endorsed by the City fans, who had crowned him as their Player of the Year, by a landslide, after the Division One championship campaign. Announcing his choice, Keegan commented: "His command of English and understanding of the game is such that he will make a very good captain. Ali's experience is unquestioned - he provides a very good link between the French-speaking players and the English ones and he leads by example. He is the greatest player in his position I have ever worked with, bar none."

High praise indeed from a man who had enjoyed a glorious career for club and country, and played alongside some fantastic talents. For Benarbia, who was also handed the hallowed No.8 jersey made famous by Colin Bell, the captaincy was the pinnacle of his time in Manchester.

He said at the time: "I know what it means to be made captain of such a great club as Manchester City and I consider it a great honour, one of the best of my career. I also know what it means to wear the No. 8 shirt and I hope I do both justice."

His relationship with the fans was one of mutual respect and admiration.

While it's common for young or mediocre footballers to praise their own supporters in a bid to curry favour, when supporters are lauded by a player with nothing to prove and who had played at the highest level of club football, it does carry extra clout.

Within weeks of his arrival in Manchester, he paid the following tribute to the fans: "The best part is playing in front of the Manchester City supporters, who are the greatest fans I have ever seen."

When asked by an interviewer if he'd ever experienced such adulation from supporters at any of his previous clubs in complete seriousness he simply said, "Yes, everywhere I go." Nobody doubted it.

The love-in between Benarbia and Manchester City was not an exclusive arrangement. Arsenal boss Wenger, no mean judge of a player's ability, spoke of Benarbia in glowing terms: "Perhaps people in this country don't know how good Ali has been over the past decade.

"He is fantastic and I would say one of the greatest passers of the ball French football has ever seen. Every year he played in the French First Division, he was top of the accuracy and assist charts. Quite simply, he can hurt you everywhere on the pitch."

As captain, he helped record signing Nicolas Anelka settle at Maine Road, and his work with younger players, particularly Shaun Wright-Phillips, is also worthy of mention.

The move up to the top flight of English football proved to be a challenge to Benarbia, by then aged 33. The extra physical demands and speed required in the Premiership meant that his contribution was limited to the occasional cameo performance and odd flash of brilliance. He scored three times in 24 outings during the 2002/03 Premiership campaign. He still had the ability to inspire his team-mates, though, coming on to turn around a home fixture against Aston Villa, and helping to feed the Goat for the equaliser at the 1-1 Old Trafford derby with a perfectly flighted free-kick.

That first season back in the Premiership saw the Blues finish in a creditable ninth position. Then, following the shocking death of City team-mate Marc Vivien Foe in the summer of 2003, and after a particularly bruising pre-season friendly at Mansfield, Benarbia initially announced his retirement from football, at least the hurly-burly world of European football.

Happily though, the beautiful game was not yet ready to wave farewell to one of its most passionate and artistic exponents, as Benarbia opted to end his career in the less physically demanding, but equally lucrative, Middle East.

Having signed for Qatari club Al-Rayyan, Benarbia obtained permission from his new employers to wave farewell to his legion of City fans by leading the club out for the first half in the stunning new City of Manchester Stadium in the friendly against Barcelona – the opening fixture in the Blues' new multi-million pound home.

He may have departed for sunnier climes, but Ali B, kept his ties with the Blues. He acts, on an informal basis, as a talent scout in the Middle East.

Despite the brevity of his time with the Blues, Benarbia will always be classed as one of City's favourite sons and some time after his departure from the club, it was clear the little Algerian will never forget his time at Maine Road.

He said: "I enjoyed two wonderful years at Manchester City. My aim when I joined was always to help the team gain promotion, and then to become established in the Premiership. I believe we did that, particularly after our ninth-placed finish in 2003. "I also wanted to finish my career on a high, knowing that I had played my best and done justice to myself and the team. My concern was that I would not be able to sustain the level required in the Premiership and that proved the case. "I enjoyed every minute of every day I was a City player and the club will be always in my heart. I follow their progress closely.

"I couldn't think of a better club at which to finish my competitive career. My thanks go out again to the Manchester City fans, who were quite honestly the most amazing I have ever played for. I hope they have every success in the world."

He scored beautiful goals, made goals for others out of nothing and was a complete joy to watch. Undoubtedly the best-ever free transfer the club has ever had, Benarbia is one of the greatest talents, and most popular, ever to have donned the famous blue shirt.

Shaun Goater

1997-2003: 216 games, 103 goals

CITY WERE IN trouble. It was March and with all the grace of a lumbering hippo attempting to climb a muddy waterhole's steep bank, the team just couldn't shake off the malaise that had enveloped them for a whole season and now threatened them with relegation. All City fans are familiar with the dreaded 'r' word, but on this particular occasion, it wasn't merely bouncing between the top flight and Division Two/Division One/The Championship (delete as applicable depending on age) that was of concern.

This was the threat of relegation to Division Three, as old timers used to know it - and whatever monicker it carries at the time of publication, it remains the nation's third tier. Read that again - Manchester City + Third Division. Think Rolling Stones + Smash Hits exclusive or Bruce Willis + *Hollyoaks* cameo. Some things just don't sound right.

Joe Royle had seemed to have enough time to turn things around, yet here they were, going into the final furlong with the kind of idle canter all racetrack punters dread, that of the dis-interested backmarker.

The corridors of Maine Road have never been paved with gold so he would have to spend what he had wisely, and with the transfer deadline looming, Royle, who shopped with confidence in the lower leagues, decided to take a punt on a player who'd once destroyed a team of his in a previous life - Oldham Athletic Reserves. For some reason that isn't blatantly clear, City fans have always refered to Latics fans as 'Yard Dogs' - if only they'd known Royle was prepared to punt the last of his kitty on a player who once had a good game against the Yard Dog Stiffs...

SHAUN GOATER HAD become a familiar name via the Sunday papers' results pages. Rarely seen on TV, he plied his trade with great effect at Rotherham United and then Bristol City. There was something different about this journeyman striker - a fact that most football fans were aware of but couldn't immediately recount. He was from Barbados? The Bahamas? Whatever, it was somewhere a damned sight more inviting that Rotherham on a damp November morning.

In fact, he was from Bermuda, an island that was famed for shorts, an area of ocean where large vessels disappeared and one of English football's first black stars, Clyde Best. A hotbed of football talent it clearly wasn't.

Leonardo Shaun Goater, however, would change that perception, to a certain degree. His is a story that borders on a modern-day fairytale and is a perfect example to anybody who refuses to give up on their dream, but to achieve his status as City's favourite modern-day player, he had to embark on a journey of self-discovery and courage that would have seen off many a hardened pro to win over a set of supporters who, in football terms, were on the verge of a nervous breakdown.

His story began in the humble surrounds of Court Street in Hamilton, capital of Bermuda. Born into a large but caring family, he was for most of his younger years an only child with his father, in typical style of one of the poorer areas of the picturesque island, little more than a puzzle and someone he would know nothing of until he was in his late teens.

"I didn't need my daddy," said Shaun. "I had my momma, aunts cousins and, the rock of the Goater family, my grandmother, Dorothy Dillon. We got along just fine and I had a happy childhood."

Civil unrest, caused by the assassination of the island's Governor meant that a four-year-old Shaun was living – and playing - in the middle of rioting youths and looters, but the Goater family reputation for strong-minded, independent women, several of whom lived at Shaun's grandmother's house on Court Street, meant that any local hoodlums or drug pushers ensured the naive kid was kept out of harm's way. Better that than feel the unbridled wrath of Dorothy Dillon or her daughters!

"We didn't have much money but my mom would always make sure I had everything I needed," recalls Shaun. "She worked hard as a housemaid in the local hotels, often having two jobs to make sure we had food on the table and clothes on our back. He soon earned the reputation as a promising young footballer, often urged on by his mother ("pass the ball to my son – he'll score the goals!") and by his teens he was playing for one of the island's best sides, North Village.

It was his prowess as a footballer that would earn him a scholarship in the USA, but a strange twist of fate was about to turn his world upside down and present an opportunity that would – controversially – offer him a path to one of the most famous clubs in the world.

"I was doing okay in my schooling but was missing home and playing football," says Shaun. "I returned to Bermuda during the Thanksgiving break and discovered Manchester United had taken a short mid-winter break to the island.

"I never thought 'this is my big chance' because I wasn't playing for anyone in particular and though I knew I was one of the more promising young players in Bermuda, I didn't know where my future lay. Football was largely a spare time activity and not something most kids aspired to earning a living from and though I watched English and NASL games on TV, there was only Clyde Best who had left Bermuda to forge a successful career in England and I knew nothing of him because it was before my time and he hardly ever came home."

Things, however, were about to change.

An alleged incident in a local nightclub and on a Thanksgiving break from college, he found himself the centre of attention when, following an exhibition match showcasing Bermuda's best young talents of which he was undoubtedly one, Manchester United invited him to England for a trial.

"I did okay in the match, " recalls Shaun. "It was a kind of pre-match entertainment before United played the national team, and I was considered one of the best young players in Bermuda, but the offer of a trial seemed almost too good to be true.

The offer of a trip to England and the chance of following his dreams of becoming a professional footballer were in conflict with his schooling, but everybody he knew and cared about agreed this was a chance too good to turn down.

He travelled to Manchester, met Alex Ferguson and did his best during his stay before flying home to begin an alternative career as a junior in a surveyor's office. He was playing for North Village again and also blossoming for the national team, and it was on one such jaunt overseas that the news he'd dreamed of and hoped for was announced.

"Several months had passed since my trial," he recalls. "I'd pretty much given up on the idea of being signed by United and then the national coach, during a team briefing blurts out 'And congratulations to Shaun Goater who has been offered a two-year deal by Manchester United' – I was like 'say what?'"

He travelled to England to begin his professional career and though the money was poor (he could earn more back home packing groceries for wealthy American tourists!) he began to learn his trade and though he did well for the youth team and reserves, when injury and suspension offered the possibility of a first-team chance, he was overlooked on several occasions.

"I watched my team-mates Lee Sharpe and Mark Robins progress, but I felt that even if I saw my two years out at United, I'd never get anywhere so when Rotherham United came in for me, I thought 'why not?'

"I hadn't a clue who they were or where they were, but after a few months at Millloor, I was still wondering if the sun ever shone in South Yorkshire."

Shaun stayed with the Millers for six years, playing in front of gates that rarely topped 6,000 and in front of a tough, working class support that was a million miles away from his beautiful home island.

"The fans wouldn't take any crap and they'd let you know if they thought you weren't pulling your weight," he says. "I remember this guy waiting by the tunnel for me as I came off at Millmoor and he was about 16-stone and covered in tattoos. 'You're ripping us off Goater' he shouted at me and I just thought 'At £400 a week, you're ripping me off!' – though self-preservation ensured I kept my observations to myself."

Financial incentives didn't exist at Rotherham and despite his goal-scoring record, they weren't prepared to up his wages and when Bristol City offered an escape route, he took it willingly and he and his wife Anita moved to a place they reckoned was as near to life in Bermuda as possible in England.

"The sun shone more, you could smell the sea and there were seagulls everywhere," he says. "We walked around town and knew it was the right place to move to. I felt happy and recharged and I think it showed in play."

Goater became a popular figure at Ashton Gate, finishing top scorer in his first season and he was flying in his second campaign and headed for Division Two as Bristol steamrollered their way to promotion.

JOE ROYLE DECIDED Goater could score the goals his misfiring side desperately needed and offered Bristol City £400,000, which they reluctantly accepted. Goater could have turned down the chance, or the club could have rightly reacted angrily and accused City of potentially railroading their promotion challenge, but this was more than just a quick cash-in. Robins boss John Ward knew this was the realisation of a dream and being a football man, he presented his star striker with the chance to follow that dream and play for a club that is still, quite rightly, considered as one of the biggest in England.

"I loved my time at Ashton Gate, but when I was told Manchester City were interested in signing me, I knew this was the move I'd been waiting for," Shaun recalled. "I had a series of forms to sign by fax but with time running out, my bloody fax machine at home broke.

"My wife Anita ushered me away and said she would sort it out, but the deadline passed without me knowing if the forms had reached City in time or even at all. I was a nervous wreck!"

The forms had reached Maine Road and Shaun was now a City player. He still hadn't actually spoken to Joe Royle up to that point, but he didn't care. It had taken nine years of hard graft to get to a club this big and this was the stage he'd been hoping for. Nothing would stand in his way from here on in. As far as the supporters of his new club were concerened, Goater was a stop-gap and no more. At under half a million quid, it was money that, if things went pear-shaped, could be readily written off, unlike players like Lee Bradbury who had cost over £2m and returned little by way of investment.

City had signed some awful players and the squad was awash with has-beens or never-weres, yet most still believed Royle could turn things around. He had to. Around 4,000 Blues made their way over the Penines to Valley Parade and there were ironic wolf whistles as Goater made a nice flick with one of his first touches. There was no bowing and no chanting his name. Like a couple on the verge of a split, the fans and team were very much part of a love-hate relationship, still eager to be in each other's company for some perverse reason. City went 1-0 up and Goater had a chance to make it 2-0 but his intelligent lob bounced just the wrong side of the post. A portly Brazillian called Edinho would inspire Bradford to score two quick goals after the break and the Bantams won 2-1. Another nail in the coffin lid and the Mancunian army travelled home angry and disappointed, yet again.

He made his debut at Bradford City and his new team were soon 1-0 up and though he almost scored with a clever lob, his neat flicks and touches were ultimately in vain as the hosts fought back to win 2-1.

Goater managed to score on his home debut against Stockport, a 4-1 victory, no less, but the fans were tired of their under-achieving players and Shaun had walked into the eye of a storm. Even at the training sessions at Platt Lane, the players were subjected to hecklers and confidence was low among the squad. Why couldn't the players show the same passion as the fans, they wondered.

"There was this guy having go at everyone, including me saying that we were rubbish and a waste of money," recalled Shaun. "All the self-belief and verve I'd arrived from Bristol with sapped away within a few weeks and I was soon as edgy as the other lads were.

"I felt the crowd were waiting for us to make mistakes, especially at home, and it was an awkward situation to be in."

The inevitable final day drama City have often found themselves in over the years meant that even if City won at Stoke, if the catachable teams above them all won, the Blues would be relegated to the third tier of English football for the first time in the club's proud history.

The fans were suspicious of Goater's talents and whether this journeyman striker was worthy of leading their team's fight against the drop. His record to that point of one goal in six games was, in their eyes, not good enough and his name synonomous with lower league successes.

This was a club who had seen the likes of Francis Lee, Mike Summerbee, Dennis Tueart, Trevor Francis and Niall Quinn lead the front line – who was Shaun Goater anyway?

City battled away at Stoke and looked a class apart at times, Goater scoring twice in a 5-2 win – but it wasn't enough. The dreaded scenario of winning being merely academic had happened and the Blues were relegated to what was then Division Two, replacing them in Division One, ironically, were Bristol City!

"Some of the lads called me and invited me to their promotion party in Bristol" says Shaun. "I went along and despite them ribbing me, saying I should have stayed where I was, I still thought City had great potential and I wanted to make my mark and show a few thousand people what I was capable of."

Though he was finding the net regularly in Division Two, he didn't feel the fans appreciated his efforts and as the team faltered in the autumn, he found himself the target of the disgruntled support.

"The goals were still going in, but if I missed a decent chance, I could feel that the fans just weren't with me," he remembered. "I knew our situation wasn't good and that the fans expected us to be running away with the league, but we were finding it hard.

"We were everybody's cup final and by Christmas there was a very real danger that we'd be spending another season at this level, which was totally unacceptable to everyone."

But things were about to get at least a little better. Shaun had been on the bench as high-flying Stoke took a 1-0 lead into half-time at Maine Road. The large Boxing Day crowd had watched their team outplayed and outfought for much of the game and were baying for blood.

"I can't say I was relishing the prospect of being part of a side that was potentially about to blow their promotion chances," he smiles, "but I never shirked from my responsibilities so when Joe said I was going on, I knew that here was a chance to play a part in something positive.

"We wanted to get in amongst it and turn this game around – and that's exactly what happened."

Shaun played a part in the equalising goal and the entire City team were flying around the pitch like men possessed – Paul Dickov and Tony Vaughan in particular just managed to stay within the laws of the game with several ferocious challenges.

City won 2-1 and the game sparked a run to the play-off final where yet more last-day drama awaited as the Blues proved that there really only is one team who can justly wear the tag of The Great Unpredictables by turning a 0-2 scoreline on 89 minutes to a penalty shoot-out victory and promotion against the luckless Gillingham. The man who had volunteered to take the fifth penalty? Shaun Goater. What might have happened had he actually been required to take that spot-kick would have either hastened his rise in popularity or potentially been his death knell at Maine Road – as it was, City's fourth spot-kick put them in an unassailable position but whatever he might have lacked in skill or ability, he more than made up for with courage.

Shaun's haul of 20 goals had won him some time, but the vast majority still expected him to be replaced by a bigger name.

Yet Goater's strike partner Paul Dickov's contribution in terms of goals was nowhere near as prolific as his, but he was very much a crowd idol and this wasn't lost on the Bermudian. He began to study Dickov's game and quickly worked out that, in Dickov's case, it was sheer endeavour and a willingness to die for the cause.

There was no such thing as a futile chase and Goater reckoned that if this is what the City fans wanted from their players, he would do likewise and whereas he'd saved much of his energy during a game in order to be sharp inside the box, now he ran down defenders, hassled keepers and put in tackles, effectively defending from the front, just as Mike Summerbee and Francis Lee had done almost 30 years before.

"It's true that I began to study Dicky's game," he says. "I wanted to know why he couldn't put a foot wrong with the supporters whereas I topped the scoring charts with little return. It soon became clear that I needed to take the aspects of his game that were missing from mine and see if that did the trick.

"Dicky was all about aggression, all-out effort and never giving up on a seemingly lost cause. I began to chase down defenders, put myself about a bit giving my all for the shirt. I had been doing what I felt was best for the team and what benefited my game prior to that, but with the added 'Dickov factor', things began to turn around."

And how.

His subtle change in style would see one of the most dramatic turnabouts in popularity ever seen at City. By the end of his second full season at Maine Road, he was a popular member of the Blues' first team and though injury ruined his first-ever campaign in the Premiership, he still finished top scorer and had proved that he could score at any level of the game.

City were relegated back to Division One in 2001 and that cost Goater's biggest fan, manager Joe Royle who had stuck by his signing through thin and thinner, his job. His replacement, Kevin Keegan decided one of his first tasks would be to off-load Goater to Wolves and the deal very nearly came off. He probably arrived with same biased view that this gangly forward with a penchant for goals from every part of his anatomy was warming the boots of another, more illustrious star as yet to be identified - and boy, did Keegan love his celebrity footballers. That the deal with Wolves didn't come off meant that both player and manager would never be entirely at ease with each other with Shaun distrustful of a man he'd admired as a player and Keegan possibly angered by his attempts to offload a popular player while everybody was enjoying their summer sunshine and he was still basking in the honeymoon period allowed to new managers - especially a manager like Kevin Keegan. There were even suggestions that the City board had refused to sanction the deal, such was the regard for the man every knew simply as 'The Goat'.

Keegan brought in players with creative flair who helped Goat's goal tally rocket to almost 20 before Christmas. Players such as , Eyal Berkovic and Ali Benarbia and that season the song 'Feed the Goat' was born, becoming perhaps one of the most popular modern-day terrace chants in Britain and making Shaun Goater a household name.

"I didn't know what they were singing at first," he smiles. "Then the lads said 'did you hear that Goat? They were singing about you.' I thought, yeah? I'm having that!"

He'd worked hard for his moment in the sun and his popularity had grown slowly. He'd overcome the boo-boys that could easily have forced out weaker characters – and had, ask Gareth and Robert Taylor, Lee Bradbury, Lee Peacock and countless others. He'd been there and been part of the club's darkest days, but he'd also been a part of helping turn things around. He'd made the City fans respect him and in time, adore him. He'd always had time for the fans on the street and never shirked his responsibilities on and off the pitch and he'd always behaved with great dignity throughout.

'Feed the Goat' would be the first of many songs as his popularity soared, though it would never be bettered, and the goals continued to fly in. He became the first City player in 30 years to top 30 goals in a season as the Blues stormed to the Division One championship, but the best was still yet to come. Having seen off the likes of George Weah and, to a ceratin extent, Paulo Wanchope and Darren Huckerby, he'd seen Jon Macken arrive at a cost of £5m and yet again he knew his place was under threat. His opportunities became less, but he refused to complain and when asked by Keegan to step in and do a job, he responded by giving it his best shot.

Partnered by £13m new signing Nicolas Anelka for the final Manchester derby at Maine Road, Goater enjoyed a rare Premiership start on what was to be the day he reached the status of deity. On 99 career goals for the Blues, the fairytale scenario and final chapter in his City career was waiting to be written and Goat didn't disappoint.

His 100th goal for the club, with the scores at 1-1, arrived when his endeavour and belief that every ball was worth chasing was rewarded ten-fold. Using the tried and tested Dickov

Method, he followed a wayward Marc Vivien Foe pass towards the byline where Gary Neville was attempting to shepherd it out. Most strikers would have given it up and pranced back towards the centre spot in readiness for the inevitable punt up field by the goalkeeper, but Goater wasn't in the category of 'most strikers'.

Neville realised the ball didn't quite have enough pace to go out, he dithered, Goat stole the ball away and headed in towards Fabien Barthez. With Maine Road on its feet to a man, he looked up and from an acute angle, expertly slotted home the ball into the back of the net to put City 2-1 up.

A total of 100 goals in the bag in the last ever derby at Maine Road, his celebration was muted and he looked focused. "I'd seen other teams go ahead against United, over-celebrate and then end up losing. I didn't want any of that. I wanted to win and make sure I didn't lose sight of the bigger picture," he explained later.

Shortly after the break he made it 101 with a deft chip over Barthez and City won this most historic game 3-1. Feed the Goat had never been sung louder and the ground reluctantly emptied to the thunderous chorus of 'Who let the Goat Out?' One man's name occupied the thoughts of the thousands of happy Blues heading home.

And there was more to come, but it never really got any better than that.

He scored an equaliser at Old Trafford in the return match just eight seconds after coming on as a sub and had a second harshly disallowed in injury time, denying City a first Old Trafford win in 29 years, but Keegan gradually phased him out of the team, just as he'd probably planned to do all along.

He wanted multi-million pound signings leading the line in his team and Shaun Goater just didn't fit the bill. He brought in the ineffective, half-fit Robbie Fowler and made it clear that Goat's future lay elsewhere. At least he had the decency to make him captain for the last game at Maine Road, but in truth, there would have been riots if he hadn't.

On the last day he ever played a competitive game for City, a clue to why the Bermudian striker became so popular could be seen in the 400 or so City fans who waited patiently out in the pouring rain after the game for their hero to emerge.

Goater signed each and every item he was asked to and didn't leave until everyone was happy. It seems, years later, that everyone has a story about Shaun Goater the man, a popular, generous and warm bloke who made time for everybody.

The City supporters love nothing more than a trier and they recognised the effort this man had put in to win them over and ultimately help the club restore itself as an established Premiership side. He scored goals off his shin, hip, chest and knee and his short-comings, such as they were, if anything endeared him even more to the fans.

Shaun Wright-Phillips

1997-2005: 182 games, 31 goals

IF THERE'S ONE thing Manchester City FC are justly proud of, it is their youth system. For years the Blues have been bringing kids through in abundance and the names of Paul Lake, Andy Hinchcliffe, Steve Redmond and David White are perfect examples of a scouting and coaching set-up at youth level that is, quite simply, second-to-none. These lads, mostly from the local surrounds, have saved the club millions of pounds in transfer fees and, in some cases, provided funds at crucial times to keep the club from sinking into serious debt.

It had been a while since a truly exceptional talent had made it through to the first team. In fact, there hadn't been a crop of talented young stars since those aforementioned stars from the City youth team that won the FA Youth Cup back in 1986 and the last black kids to really scale the heights were keeper Alex Williams who emerged from Joe Corrigan's shadow in the late Seventies and defender Clive Wilson, a skilful midfielder/full-back from the early 1980s.

In the late 1990s, however, looking towards the future, City set up an Academy – a more professionally run and better funded youth set-up aimed at grooming kids from a variety of age groups up through the ranks until they were either deemed ready for reserve and then, hopefully, first team football – or released. It would take time and patience, but with the right scouting system, personnel and planning, there was no reason why it couldn't be a success and the Blues were among the country's pioneers in the creation of club Academies. The question was who would be the first graduate to make it through to the first team – and more to the point, would he survive and prosper or wither and fade? Only time would tell...

"HE'LL NEVER MAKE it. He's too small... let the lad go." Words that still haunt the youth coaches at Nottingham Forest a decade or so on and rightly so. Standing at 5ft 3in, Shaun Wright-Phillips clearly had ability, but the Forest staff – pardon the pun - just couldn't see past his lack of inches, despite him spending three years in the East Midlands. True, only a handful of footballers who were this height or less ever managed to carve out successful careers for themselves, but they didn't count on the size of Shaun's heart and ambition and coupled with determination, raw skill and speed, he was quite a prospect.

Still, he was released along with his brother Bradley and the pair could easily have drifted out of the game and into obscurity, but a Forest scout recommended the Wright-Phillips brothers to Manchester City and ironically, it was Bradley in particular who he ear-marked for future stardom.

City gave the brothers a trial and after seeing enough ability in the pair to work with, signed Shaun on the morning of his 17th birthday. He was nicknamed 'Rubber Man' by the kids he grew up with in and around Bermondsey, in essence, but some believe he was more of an insurance policy to secure Bradley's signature, such was the glowing praise his younger brother had arrived with at Platt Lane. With Shaun and Bradley still in their teens, it would be a few years before Academy bosses would know if the gamble of signing both boys on was going to pay off.

But there was early media interest in Shaun's progress as reports began to filter out that legendary Arsenal striker Ian Wright was Shaun's adopted father, and also Bradley's natural father. Shaun made a video appearance, looking a little shy to say the least, when Wright senior was presented with the 'Big Red Book' on *This Is Your Life* and it raised his profile a little higher. Ian Wright was still a huge name in English football at the time and City fans were keen to learn more about the young midfielder with such impressive pedigree. What kind of player was he? Was he or wasn't he Ian Wright's natural son? If so was he likely to follow in his dad's footsteps and if not, what was his background prior to adoption, if that's what happened?

In fact, the truth is Ian Wright moved in with Shaun's mother Sharon when he was just 17, prior to his stardom and Sharon was bringing up her son Shaun alone. Ian and Sharon had a child between them, Bradley, but Shaun and Ian had always considered each other father and son – Shaun wasn't adopted in the sense most people imagine.

Occasional news features popped up in the local press and it became noticeable that the numbers watching the home youth matches had increased as Shaun's reputation as an exciting prospect steadily grew. Shaun was progressing well and to the City coaches it was abundantly clear that in this case, size really didn't matter. Joe Royle arrived to become the latest City manager in early 1998 following Frank Clark's dismissal and during his first training session he commented that 'the little fella on the wing was terrific'. Shaun had caught his eye immediately and he would now need to show the same appetite in every training session, youth match or reserve game if he was to win a longer contract and give himself a crack at making it into the first-team.

In fact, Royle wasted little time in giving the 17-year-old his debut as a second-half substitute at Burnley in the Worthington Cup. He replaced Terry Cooke and after a 1-0 win (6-0 on aggregate), Royle said: "This was a good game to introduce him to the first team and he showed glimpses of what he can do.

"Shaun is only 17 and he is a precocious talent. Certainly one for the future."

Royle gradually introduced the teenager into the senior squad, much to the delight of the City fans, many of whom had taken a vested interest in his progress and he made an impressive second-half display away to Port Vale, claiming to have scored the winning goal – though the 'experts' decided it was to be credited as an own goal – as if the defender wanted it!

Royle said after that: "Shaun is as brave as a lion and could turn out to be anything he wants. He's lightning quick and gives us a new dimension. I will tread a little warily with him because he is only young, but he had definitely given me something to think about."

For his part, Shaun said: "People talk about my size but it doesn't bother me. I have quick feet and hopefully a quick brain and I play with my heart. I don't care how big the opposition is – I'll take them on."

IF THERE WAS a script that had to be read to make himself a crowd favourite, Wright-Phillips learned it off by heart. He made his full senior bow a week later during a 4-2 win over Portsmouth. He received a tremendous backing from the 31,660 Maine Road crowd and to begin your career in the senior side knowing that everyone was willing you to succeed must have been a huge fillip for the teenager. He was also coming into a side with a winning mentality as Royle's team chased back-to-back promotions from Division Two to the Premiership.

To have crowd backing like that is as much as any teenager dare hope for, but it wasn't just down to the fact he was 'Ian Wright's boy', as he was labelled at every opportunity in the media. The story of Forest releasing him because of his size has endeared the player to the supporters perhaps even more – Blues fans have always been suckers for a hard luck story or somebody who is having a difficult time. The role of the underdog has been almost engineered into the club's DNA due to the success of

United over the years. In fact, the club has been positively drawn to players like George Best, who the club tried to sign when he attempted a comeback from retirement despite his walking out on Manchester United and having well-documented alcohol and gambling problems – Shaun, it's worth noting, had no such problems.

"I don't want to talk about my dada because I don't want to be known as Ian Wright's son," said Shaun in an early interview back in 1999. "I'm my own player. He inspires me – because he's my dada – but I don't want to be just known as his son."

His dad Ian added: "Shaun will always carry the burden of having me as his dad and I think he's found the media attention hard to handle already. But he will realise he has to overcome bigger hurdles than that if he wants to be a top professional. I'm very proud of him."

Shaun even dropped the 'Wright' off the back off his shirt for a while and was plain old Phillips, before he realised it didn't really matter. He played again in a 1-1 draw with QPR a week after his full debut, but despite appearing on the bench several times later in the season, Royle opted for experience as his side won promotion on the last day of the campaign.

Over the next two years, Wright-Phillips would feature more and more with the fans loving his electrically-charged runs down the right, but it wasn't just his offensive play that they admired - he was prepared to get stuck in and work hard for the team and away from the pitch he was quiet and unassuming. His dribbling ability, matched with his low sense of gravity meant he was a real problem for defenders and his pace was an added bonus. He was tough, too, and literally would bounce back up if clattered and rode challenges that would put others in hospital.

Royle gave him his Premiership debut on the opening day of the 2000/01 season, but he came off the bench with the team already well on their way to a disastrous 4-0 defeat at Charlton Athletic.

George Weah and Paulo Wanchope had been signed on the eve of the season and Wright-Phillips got to play alongside Weah on just one occasion before the Liberian legend fell out with the manager and quit Maine Road. He became a regular on the bench for the remainder of the campaign, but again, Royle opted for experience as his team battled to stay in the Premiership, ultimately failing.

When he did play, his durability impressed not only the City fans, but also his dad, who, during one televised match, winced as Shaun was the subject of a horror tackle by the corner flag. Ian Wright, a pundit for the televised game watched the replay of the foul during the half-time break and casually said, 'Oh, he's all right. His legs are made of rubber.' Gradually, he lost the tag of 'Ian Wright's son' and became Shaun Wright-Phillips, possibly for the first time in his life, he was standing on his own two feet and wasn't being judged on who his father was and what he'd achieved in the game. He had also etched his name into a long list of black players who had progressed through the ranks, hardly surprising, perhaps, for a club who had been based in the heart of Moss Side and its predominantly black community for 80 years. Clive Wilson, Alex Williams, Dave Bennett and Roger Palmer were four such talents plucked from the local populace who went on to become huge crowd favourites at Maine Road.

Wright-Phillips was making his own path, though and though he made several appearances under Royle, most were from the substitutes' bench and he didn't find the net during his first few seasons. When Royle was controversially sacked in May 2001, new boss Kevin Keegan confidently predicted his young charge would one day play for England one day and he would make the 21-year-old who didn't seem capable of turning in a below par performance, a permanent fixture in his side. But there was still one thing missing from his game – goals – they would, however, be well worth waiting for when they did eventually come.

TELLINGLY, KEEGAN NAMED Wright-Phillips in his side in only his third match in charge and he also introduced the youngster to the sublime midfield talents of Eyal Berkovic and Ali Benarbia to further his education and the endless training sessions with the two foreign visionaries made his touch surer, his mind sharper and his creativity levels rocketed. He was rarely out of the squad and the fans loved seeing him in the team. He was a box-of-tricks player in a side brimming with confidence and invention. He knew he could try anything in such exalted company and he was revelling in it, though never cocky or arrogant.

When promotion-chasing City travelled to Millwall in November 2001, they did so with no travelling fans due to crowd trouble during previous meetings at both clubs' grounds. Shaun Goater and Wright-Phillips in particular were subjected to a barrage of racist abuse during the Division One clash at the New Den, but on this occasion, it was the young City midfielder who would have the last laugh.

Driving forward with the scores level at 2-2 and just minutes remaining, Wright-Phillips drove forward and unleashed a 20-yard scorcher that rocketed into the roof of the net to win the game and shove the racist chants back down the throats of the idiots who had made them. How sweet to open your account in such a hostile environment and it further showed the courage of the 20-year-old – typical that there were no City fans for him to celebrate with! It didn't stop him, Goater and Darren Huckerby running to the empty away fans end and applauding the vacant seats as though they were filled with thousands of dancing Mancunians. Genius!

The mental shackles released, this would be the first of many spectacular goals for the rising star and he'd finally found the missing piece of his personal jigsaw. Keegan had assembled a fantastic side of attacking players, full of creativity and invention and the Blues were well on their way to winning the Division One title in a canter. Keegan then employed him as an attacking wing-back, playing him for the majority of games after Christmas and it was Wright-Phillips' two goals at promotion rivals Wolves in April 2002 that all but secured the Blues' place back in the nation's elite. He ran to the City fans and lifted up his shirt to show the message 'The Wright Stuff' on a white T-shirt beneath but he was only preaching to the converted. The fans adored his whole-hearted, down-to-earth approach to football and with the mega-bucks arrival of Nicolas Anelka as City kicked off the 2002/03 campaign, he would again be learning from one of the best in Europe.

While Anelka was moody and sullen, 'Wrighty' was bubbly and enthusiastic, playing with a smile on his face and enjoying himself, probably because he was all too aware of how easily he might have slipped out of football altogether just a few years before. He was both exciting and hard-working and the supporters loved the fact that he'd proved the doubters wrong and had been nurtured as one of their own. He simply could do no wrong and in Keegan, he'd found a manager who let him run free, do his own thing and believed fully in his abilities. He scored his first Premiership goal in 25 attempts, against Fulham, seconds after coming on as a sub, though it would prove to be his only goal of the season.

By the start of 2003/04, he was almost the sole creative force in the side, following Benarbia's exit and Berkovic's fall-out with Keegan. The teamsheet was almost unthinkable without his name on it and he took to the added weight of expectation like the proverbial duck to water. The disappointing Steve McManaman paled into insignificance against Wright-Phillips' all-action displays and with other overpaid stars such as Robbie Fowler failing to produce the goods, time and time again it was SWP who the fans compared all others to. He scored twice that season against Manchester United, once at Old Trafford and then a spectacular last-minute effort that crashed in off the underside of the crossbar to complete a 4-1 rout in the first City of Manchester Stadium derby. 'Shauny Wright-Wright-Wright!' had never been sung louder.

He was also a player who transcended traditional rivalries and was genuinely popular and admired around the country. When he came on for his England debut against Ukraine in September 2003, he received a terrific reception and minutes later he'd scored a typical low drive from distance.

At club level he was the beating heart of the team, with the effervescent inspiration who could score goals from nothing and bring the crowd to their feet in a way that few had managed in the past 30 years or so. In a team that had a number of crowd favourites, it was Wright-Phillips who was the most popular and when club legend Shaun Goater left, he became even more important to the fans.

Yet fame came at a price, and City fans knew their jewel would some day probably leave, the subject of some ridiculous offer or other. He continued to play for England and when he penned a new four-year contract just after the 2004/05 season began, the supporters breathed a collective sigh of relief. "Why would I want to leave?" he claimed. "This is my home."

THINGS WERE GOING well and Wright-Phillips understandably didn't seem to want to change the course of his destiny. In September 2004 he even started up front with younger brother Bradley and pulled the strings throughout a stunning display that saw City triumph 7-1 over Barnsley. Then, the interest seemed to crank up a notch.

Spurs tested the water with a bid of £5m – hopeful at best – and Chelsea and Arsenal were constantly linked with huge bids for his services. The Arsenal interest was understandable – Shaun was a boyhood Gunners fan, a native Londoner and his dad was a Highbury legend, so it was extra special for everyone at City when he scored a fantastic goal in front of the North Bank in January 2005 to earn the Blues a rare point in North London. As some of Keegan's expensive flops faded into obscurity, Wright-Phillips was arguably the country's most coveted talent and it seemed just a matter of time before he would leave and join a side challenging for Champions League glory – this is what all footballers, we are told, strive for. Keegan finally left his post in March 2005, feeling his influence and motivational skills had waned to the point of hindrance and Stuart Pearce took the reins.

City emerged from their late winter malaise and strung together a remarkable run of results, inspired by – who else? Shaun Wright-Phillips. A magnificent solo goal at Aston Villa helped spearhead the Blues' dramatic late push for Europe, but few realised it would also be his last in a City shirt. The Blues were within a victory of a UEFA Cup place and with the scores 1-1 against Middlesbrough, who only needed a draw to secure the final European spot, but Robbie Fowler's injury-time miss from the penalty spot cost the Blues dearly and if Wright-Phillips had wanted to pit his wits against some of the best in Europe for the second time in three years, his hopes were dashed again and put on hold for another year at least.

The summer months passed with speculation that Chelsea were about to make a bid reaching fever pitch in the national media, hungry for a major story to fill their pages. Incredibly, Arsenal boss Arsene Wenger publicly stated that he wished Chelsea would hurry up and put in an offer for Wright-Phillips because the whole saga was becoming frustrating for him – bloody cheek! Wenger's total lack of disrespect towards Manchester City was incredible, but the comments passed by with little reaction.

Wright-Phillips returned for pre-season training still a City player and with three years on his contract to run. Now a regular in Sven-Goran Ericksson's England squad, all he had to do was continue doing what he'd been doing for his club for another 10 months and he'd be on his way to the World Cup in Germany and a chance to show a global audience of millions what he could do.

But then, the inevitable happened. Chelsea, whose attitude to the whole affair had been a tad blasé to say the least, finally lodged a massive bid of £20m.

It was an incredible offer and one the City board, to their great credit, turned down. Shaun stated he didn't want to leave City and his legion of supporters breathed a collective sigh of relief. He played against Tranmere in a pre-season friendly and happily signed autographs and posed for photographs – all was well in the world and City fans lauded the fact that their club had been the one that stood up against the arrogant Londoners and their bottomless bank account, fat cheques and cocky manager, but the following day, Wright-Phillips pulled out of a friendly with Macclesfield citing a stomach bug as the reason. He then informed City chairman John Wardle that he had decided he now wanted to talk to Chelsea.

Whatever happened during those 24 hours to change his mind may never be known, but as far as the City fans were concerned, that was that. Chelsea returned with a bid of £21m, which was accepted and Shaun signed a mega-money deal with the Premiership champions. Some supporters blamed his agent Mitchell Thomas, while others pointed the finger squarely at his step dad Ian Wright, who had made murmurings before – or at least had been attributed to comments suggesting his son deserved a bigger stage than the one Manchester City were giving him.

No amount of money could appease the crestfallen supporters who had lost their idol. The little kid deemed to have no future as a junior and the flag bearer of by now the most envied Academy in the country had just fetched in a transfer fee some £14m greater than any previously the club had received and, in doing so, considerably eased the sizeable club debt.

Of course, he would now terrorise Europe through the Champions League and inspire England to World Cup glory, or so we thought. In an incredible twist of fortune, Chelsea boss Jose Mourinho used his new signing only occasionally and Wright-Phillips' confidence visibly sapped as he was continually left on the bench and when he did play, he seemed a shadow of the player that had terrorised the Premiership for several years.

His self-belief seemed dented and the idolising supporters had been replaced by nervy cameos in front of fans used to seeing the best thanks to a whole squad of superstars.

The biggest bombshell of all, however, awaited him at the end of his first season with the champions and as Sven-Goran Eriksson suddenly discovered a new Russian roulette attitude to his squad selection, Wright-Phillips was sensationally left out of the England World Cup party, along with Tottenham's Jermain Defoe.

The feeling of the City fans was, it's fair to say, mixed. Some, still hurting and angry that he'd left reckoned it was just desserts. But the majority felt sad that the footballer with the heart of a lion, one of their own in their eyes, had missed a trip to the greatest football show on Earth and there are certainly no guarantees he will ever get another opportunity. Hopefully, he will.

Going into the 2006/07 campaign, Wrighty was being used even more infrequently and the general view seemed to be that he would need to leave Chelsea in order to get his career back on track. City made three attempts to bring him 'home' on loan, but at the time of writing, a couple of London clubs seemed to be favourites to sign him on a permanent deal. A unique talent who enjoyed a unique relationship with the Manchester City fans. How, on occasion, he must yearn for such, belief and love once more. That, of course, of a genuine Cult Hero.

Sergio Aguero

2011-to date: 50 games, 30 goals
(as of 10th September 2012)

FOR 13 LONG years, one goal and one goal alone stood out as the club's most dramatic and most crucial. Paul Dickov's last-minute strike against Gillingham in the 1999 play-off final not only revived City's hopes of promotion, but altered the landscape of the decade and more to follow. The Blues' long awaited return to the Premier League, their ventures into European football and even the club's 2011 FA Cup success all stemmed back to that historic Wembley equaliser.

Yet just as the Class of '68 were finally consigned to the file entitled 'Happy Memories' on the final day of the 2011/12 season, as was Dickov's goal superseded in City folklore by arguably the most important strike in Premier League history. Roberto Mancini's side had needed a hero in the dying seconds of that meeting with Queens Park Rangers and it was Sergio Aguero's head that appeared over the parapet as the Argentinean striker earned the status of Cult Hero by changing scenes of despair into euphoric celebrations in a matter of moments.

Just ten months earlier, one of Europe's most sought-after talents, Aguero had arrived at the Etihad Stadium. His reputation had been garnered in his native Argentina before a move to Spain provided him with a European stage on which to shine. Despite proving his worth in La Liga for Atletico Madrid, the success of local rivals Real and Catalan giants Barcelona meant that Aguero often struggled to escape the mighty shadows cast by Cristiano Ronaldo and Lionel Messi. A move to Manchester would change all of that, however, and at a cost in excess of £30m, City fought off the late advances of Real and Chelsea to secure his signature. City fans had no idea just how invaluable Aguero would prove over the course of his first season with the club.

Born and raised as one of seven children in the modest Argentine province of Quilmes, Aguero joined South American giants Independiente at the age of nine. It was here that his raw talent and natural ability were nurtured and after working his way through the club's youth ranks – being fast-tracked to play with boys two years older than him – Aguero burst on to the first-team scene aged just 15 years and 35 days in July 2003. In doing so, the gifted teenager became the youngest player to ever appear in the Argentine Premier League – a record previously held by football legend Diego Maradona, Aguero's future father-in-law. Made to wait seven months before returning to the Independiente starting line-up, a string of impressive performances eventually cemented his place in the first XI. Affectionately nicknamed 'Kun' due to his resemblance to a Japanese anime character, he ensured he would never be forgotten by his first club when he ran from the halfway line to score a spectacular goal against local rivals Racing Club de Avellaneda. Selection for the 2005 FIFA U20 World Cup offered Aguero the platform on which to impress the world and despite only making a number of cameos as Argentina secured World Cup glory, eyes from abroad were soon cast in the teenager's direction.

Twelve months later, Atletico Madrid parted with a club record 20 million euros in order to capture Aguero's signature. The dominance of Real Madrid and Barcelona was something that

Atletico had fought for years and although Aguero would never lift the La Liga title at the Vicente Calderon, the Spanish club hoped that a partnership with the club's resident icon Fernando Torres would provide them with their own slice of success. Instead, Aguero was gradually eased into European football by manager Javier Aguirre – scoring just six goals as Atletico finished the campaign in seventh – before Torres departed for the Premier League. In truth, it was only when Torres joined Liverpool that a 19-year-old Aguero flourished. Some 12 months after making his senior international debut against Brazil, his performances in a second FIFA U20 World Cup saw him take centre stage as the fledgling teenager was named Player of the Tournament. A tally of six goals in seven games epitomised the Golden Boot winner's impressive tournament and he returned to La Liga with a second international title to his name.

With European qualification ensured via the Intertoto Cup and a new strike partner in Uruguayan Diego Forlan, Kun excelled at Atletico and was recognised as the FIFA World Young Player of the Year in 2007. The South American pairing combined to create a formidable strike-force and with 19 league goals, club top-scorer Aguero led the Spanish outfit to Champions League qualification for the first time in a decade. His man-of-the-match performance and two-goal haul against Barcelona in a 4-2 win in March 2008 won him the plaudits of the Spanish media and his side's fourth-place finish signalled the start of a new era for Atletico. Aguero's remarkable form saw him awarded with the Trofeo EFE – recognition of the most impressive Ibero-American Player of the Year. Incredibly, he was the only player other than compatriot Lionel Messi to win the award between 2006 and 2012. A call to represent Argentina alongside future City team-mate Pablo Zabaleta at the 2008 Beijing Olympics followed. Unable to replicate his goalscoring exploits of the summer before, Aguero crucially found the net twice against Brazil in the semi-finals and eventually added Olympic Gold to his already impressive record of achievements.

Club team-mate Forlan would take the lead as Atletico's most prolific striker upon Aguero's return to domestic action during the 2008/09 campaign, but the Olympic champion's tireless work ethic and outstanding attitude off the field continued to earn rave reviews. The Argentinean's first foray into Europe's elite competition would bear fruit in the form of three goals and progress through a tricky group into the second round. Porto would prove an eventual stumbling block to Los Colchoneros' European ambitions, but their excellent league form ensured a second consecutive season of Champions League football for Aguero in which he would first attract the attention of English clubs. Two goals over two legs contributed to Atletico's qualification at the expense of Greek side Panathinaikos as Chelsea lay in wait in the group stages. Kun's brace earned his side an ultimately fruitless point against the London club as Atletico failed to progress and were instead relegated to the Europa League despite his outstanding displays.

Initial disappointment aside, the often overlooked Madrid club embarked on an exciting Europa League campaign. Having seen off Turkish giants Galatasaray in the round of 32, Aguero was called upon to book Atletico's place in the quarter-finals. Competing with Sporting Lisbon for a place in the last eight, Kun and co. struggled to find a way past the Portuguese outfit in the home leg of the round, ensuring that the odds were stacked against them going into the second leg. Dependable as ever, Aguero scored twice as his side progressed on goal difference. Valencia and Liverpool also fell victim to the away goals rule as Atletico booked their place in the Europa League Final at their expense. Up against a fantastic Fulham side, the eyes of the Premier League were watching. Former United striker Forlan may have scored the goals that won the tournament, but Aguero's creative presence caused a rush of Premier League interest in the Argentinean ace ahead of the 2010 World Cup.

Having achieved incredible success with the youth national squads throughout his career, Aguero was selected by father-in-law Diego Maradona to represent the South American outfit on the senior international stage. Far from being an established member of the first team, Kun made his World Cup debut in the second group stage game against South Korea and started for Argentina as they recorded a third win from three in the final group game against Greece. Relegated to the bench for his country's round of 32 win over Mexico, Aguero was helpless to prevent Argentina's last-eight exit from the competition when he entered the fray in the 75th minute of his side's 4-0 drubbing at the hands of Germany. Chelsea, Tottenham and Real Madrid were all suitably impressed with the striker's potential and were linked with moves that subsequently never materialised as Aguero remained on the continent for a season that would ultimately be his last.

Atletico's 2010 European adventure had taken its toll on their league form and seen them finish ninth in La Liga – their lowest position since Aguero's arrival. Only on the strength of their Europa League success the season before had his side qualified for any form of European competition and though Kun remained loyal to the Spanish side, those around the club knew that Champions League qualification was a must if they hoped to hang on to their most capable star beyond the 2010/11 campaign. Despite Sergio's best efforts, his side would only manage seventh. It was arguably Aguero's best season in the red and white of Atletico; netting 20 league goals for the first time in his career and scoring a first career hat-trick during his final ever appearance for the club, Aguero could have done little else to improve his side's league standing or prevent their disastrous exit from the group stages of the Europa League.

Following a successful Copa America – in which he scored three goals in four games before Argentina were dumped out of the quarter-finals by eventual winners Uruguay – Aguero found his name top of every wish-list amongst Europe's elite. His inevitable move away from the Vicente Calderon came in July 2011 when City made their move for one of world football's hottest properties. Like so many of the Blues' other high profile signings over the preceding years, capturing Kun's signature was far from easy but when the Atletico striker arrived at the Etihad to iron out the finer details of his transfer on 27 July 2011, the City faithful that gathered left Sergio with no doubt as to which club he should join. Hundreds of fans congregated outside the stadium for as long as seven hours in eager anticipation of Aguero's appearance and when he eventually arrived, he was given the most rapturous reception. In response, the City new-boy made the ultimate first impression by remaining outside to sign every autograph and have as many photos as the supporters requested. He later claimed it was his reward to fans for greeting him in such an incredible fashion. Aguero displayed the modesty and humility born out of his humble beginnings and the Blues' support lapped it up.

Upon completing his club record move to Manchester, City's new number 16 explained that he had joined the club in a bid to compete at the top and with the aim of building a legacy on the club's 2010 FA Cup success. Cut from the same cloth as City skipper Carlos Tevez, Aguero's arrival proved timely as speculation linking the Blues' 2010/11 top scorer with a move away from the club continued to busy the journalists. Aware that his compatriot may soon be on his way, Aguero assured fans that he was capable of performing no matter who he lined up alongside and instantly dismissed suggestions that he would need time to settle into the English game. City star David Silva had taken months to truly find his feet in the Premier League after joining from La Liga club Valencia but Aguero had no such qualms – how right he was as he made a debut to remember on the opening day of the 2011/12 season.

Newly promoted Swansea visited the Etihad and with manager Roberto Mancini having rested his record signing for the Community Shield defeat against United one week earlier, fans were foaming at the mouth at the prospect of finally seeing Kun in action. Left out of the starting line-up once again, Blues were left to wait a further hour before their new hero joined the action. How he was worth the wait! Scoring after just eight minutes to double City's advantage, Aguero was majestic in the way that he created the third goal for David Silva and completed his incredible debut by scoring a stunning goal from long range. Kun had arrived and Mancini had seemingly pulled off a masterstroke as fears of a possible Tevez exit were allayed in 30 short minutes. Scorer of eight goals in his first five league games for the club, Aguero wasn't just proving an incredible pick by those who had included him in their fantasy football teams but was leading the way in City's title charge.

Intent on challenging for the title, the father-of-one had also joined City to make a return to Champions League football. His two previous experiences of the competition had only served to whet the appetite of the 2010 Europa League winner and he hoped to make a splash in the Blues' inaugural year. A draw with Napoli and that infamous defeat in Munich effectively passed Aguero by, but when the Blues were most in need, Kun made his mark. At home to Spanish outfit Villarreal in the crucial third game of the group stages, City required no less than three points or a miracle to follow in the second round of group fixtures. A slice of luck pulled Mancini's side level having fallen behind in the opening stages of the game, but with 90 minutes on the clock, the Blues were in dire need of one more goal. Up stepped Aguero. His last-gasp strike not only sent 40,000 City fans into a frenzy but also manager Roberto Mancini, who couldn't hide his joy by celebrating in frantic style – a reaction that would be matched only by a certain other Aguero goal on the closing day of the Premier League season.

In the absence of Carlos Tevez – who had fallen out with Mancini and returned to Argentina – Sergio Aguero became the focal point of the Blues' vast array of attacking talent. Aguero's performances on the field and temperament away from it had him establishing a place in the hearts of the City faithful. Despite having found the net in the 6-1 drubbing of United, scored a goal in the first minute of the Europa League meeting with Portuguese giants Porto and been named Etihad Player of the Year prior to that fateful final day of the season, Aguero's season was far from over.

Not for 42 years had the Blues been crowned champions and for far too long City had wavered in the shadow of their arch-rivals. On 13 May 2012, however, everything changed as Sergio Aguero defied the odds in the dying moments of the final day of the 2011/12 season. Going into the game, City were overwhelming favourites. They had somehow clawed back an eight-point deficit between themselves and Sir Alex Ferguson's United to sit atop the Premier League on goal difference and as long as the Blues could overcome former manager Mark Hughes and his Queens Park Rangers side, the title was theirs. Pablo Zabaleta's goal gave City a vital half-time lead and the title chase looked done and dusted. Few expected Djibril Cisse's equaliser; even less expected the goal that looked set to condemn Blues to another year of hurt as Jamie Mackie put QPR 2-1 ahead. The clock ran down and even when Edin Dzeko equalised with only stoppage time left, it just seemed too much to believe that City could actually win this. What was to come was inconceivable just moments earlier but as Aguero received a return pass from Balotelli and beat the final QPR defender, the Argentinean secured his place in Premier League history by finding the net to win his side the title and condemn the phrase 'typical City' to the history books forever.

Two images would become synonymous with that moment. While the Etihad exploded with a roar of jubilation, Aguero wheeled away in celebration, spinning his shirt over his head. Though most Blues were enjoying the moment far too much to notice their hero's irrepressible reaction to the most important goal of his career, that celebration would be watched time and time again by City fans throughout the world on television screens and over the internet. Captain Vincent Kompany later claimed that the title-winning striker had shed tears of delight as his team-mates had piled on top of him and that's something that Blues will never forget. Aguero had made the dreams of every single City supporter come true in the most dramatic style imaginable. Not only had Kun won City the title, but he had robbed United of a 20th in the most devastating fashion.

During the mass ecstasy that followed, one television commentator claimed that "you will never see anything like this again!" and it would take something very special to top the conclusion to Aguero's first ever season in the Premier League. During the last great City glory era, the Maine Road faithful had hailed Colin Bell as the King of the Kippax. Surrounded by the likes of Mike Summerbee, Mike Doyle and Francis Lee, Colin Bell was revered as the Blues' greatest player.

Today, with a new Cult Hero to worship, City fans are already wondering if Sergio could be the most talented player to ever wear sky blue. And the best thing is, he will only get better...